Hokkaido
Sea of Japan
Sado
Sendai
Hekura
The Seven Islands
Wajima
Noto Peninsula
Nanao
Honshu
Kanazawa
Tokyo
Kamakura
Atami
Boso Peninsula
Kyoto
shima
Kobe
Nara
Onjuku
Osaka
Toba
Hatsushima
Miura Peninsula
Izu Peninsula
Shikoku
u
Pacific Ocean
0
50
100 Miles

# *The Island of the Fisherwomen*

*By the same Author*

SECRET TIBET

MEETING WITH JAPAN

KARAKORAM: THE ASCENT OF GASHERBRUM IV

# *The Island of the Fisherwomen*

BY
FOSCO MARAINI

TRANSLATED FROM THE ITALIAN
BY
ERIC MOSBACHER

HARCOURT, BRACE & WORLD, INC., NEW YORK

*first American edition 1962*

*Published in Italy under the title* L'Isola delle Pescatrici *and in England under the title* Hekura: The Diving Girls' Island

*Library of Congress Catalog Card Number: 62-10498*
*Illustrations printed in Italy*
*Text printed in the United States of America*

# Contents

# *The Island of the Fisherwomen*

# Bundles, Babies, and Behinds

THERE was now no more doubt that we really were going to Hekura. Preparations had lasted a week. The underwater filming equipment had to be got ready, and tents and camping equipment procured in case we failed to find a house to live in; and above all, as nobody seemed to know anything about Hekura, there were a great many lacunae of information to be filled in. The three original members of the little expedition were Mr. Murata, a smiling but stubborn little man who was to be our producer, Takahashi, the young assistant camera-man, and myself. But at the last moment we were joined by Penny, an adventure-loving American girl, who insisted on missing absolutely nothing in Japan.

On July 24th Tokyo lay under a blinding white haze; it was one of those sweltering Japanese summer days when the heat is enough to lay you out. I do not know by what miracle we succeeded in finishing all our packing at the last moment, and cramming our eighteen articles of luggage into two taxicabs. We were to meet Penny at 8.45 p.m., but there was a misunderstanding and we wasted a precious quarter of an hour. The consequence was a wild drive through the crowded streets to Ueno. Fortunately Tokyo traffic is naturally chaotic; our drivers took advantage of the chaos to cross the city like a flash.

At Ueno there was the usual tremendous crowd. Ueno is the station for the whole of north Japan. The north of Japan, like the south of Italy, is a land of poor and hungry peasants. If in Italy Christ stopped at Eboli, in Japan the Buddha stopped at Sendai. In north Japan the winter is long, the rice sometimes fails to ripen, the forests are thick and endless, and there still prevail the poverty and ignorance which with us are confined to the bare and arid mountains and torrent-swept valleys of Lucania and Calabria. The crowd at Ueno is of a special kind; there is a patient, child-like, dazed quality about it. Ueno is the only place in Tokyo in which there is such a thing as a smell of humanity. That is because there are too many people there, and perhaps not all of them have had time to wash.

Our cabs put us down just four minutes before the train left, and about those hectic few minutes I remember nothing at all; it was like being involved in an accident or a quarrel, and everything happened in a kind of daze. No doubt we grabbed some *akabo* ('red caps' or porters) and forced our way through the dense throng by the sheer weight of our persons and our eighteen articles of baggage, nearly all of which were big and some of which were pointed. We must have been extremely ruthless in forcing our way through the dense throng of torpid and bovine northern peasants, but it was impossible to explain.

However, we managed it. Our pile of baggage was deposited safely in the last carriage; and at 9.19 precisely we collapsed on top of it, exhausted.

At Ueno even the trains are different from those at other Tokyo stations. They move off straining and panting, as if the effort were almost too much for them, and they howl through the night like wolves on the steppe; they suggest some sort of human monster complaining at having to make yet another agonizing journey hundreds of miles through ravine and mountain. The trains are always crowded to bursting point; travelling in them is like taking part in a mass flight, a migration; and a trail of weeping women is always left behind on the platform.

During the night we had to make our way along the whole length of the train, because the sleeping-car in which places were reserved for us was next to the engine. What a job it was! Japanese railway carriages consist of single compartments only; every square inch of usable space was occupied, and everyone was asleep. A mass of humanity were clustered on the seats, on the floor and even in the luggage racks. The scene might have been conceived by Doré, Dante's illustrator; we were confronted with an inextricable medley of arms, heads, legs, shoes, bundles, babies and behinds. The ability of the Japanese to adapt themselves to the most adverse circumstances, and to find in them not only peace, but dignity, is certainly unique in the world.

From Tokyo to the Sea of Japan is a long way—it is over four hundred miles to Wajima at the northern extremity of the Noto peninsula. Japanese trains, except on the Tokaido, between Tokyo and Osaka, are very slow. It took us fifteen hours to reach our destination; thus our average speed was about thirty miles an hour. However, we had to cross all the mountains of the provinces of Gumma and Niigata, that is to say, the Alpine backbone of the chief island of the Japanese archipelago.

At Tsubata—not far from the town of Kanazawa, a famous centre of culture of the Tokugawa period—we left the main line and took a quiet little train in which we crossed the countryside of the Noto peninsula. Here our average speed must have been roughly that of a stage-coach. But what was the hurry? The sky had cleared, and all round us were paddy-fields, woods, lakes, clusters of houses each more beautiful then the last; and from time to time we caught sight of inlets of the sea. Every now and again our engine put on a crazy burst of speed down a short incline, only to be brought up again by the gentle incline opposite, up which it fought its way, gasping and panting as if about to expire. At the innumerable stations, at every one of which we stopped, plenty of time was allowed for all the innumerable necessary operations to be carried out, and there was a great movement of peasants and fishermen, merchandise and mail. The crowds were colourful in appearance and clothing, gay, calm, and in continual motion, and there were continual exchanges of greetings and little family ceremonies.

When we reached half-way at Nanao, a great fishing centre, the sea and many little islands filled the horizon. At about midday we reached our first destination, Wajima.

# Too Many Sailors

But what was the object of our little expedition? Why were we engaging in this trip?

Hekura* is a small island, and it still seemed very far away. We were going there because it was a home of the Ama, and the Ama are children of the sea. We had been on their trail for a long time. Meanwhile we had got as far as Wajima, where the land ends, and in front of us the blue sea beat noisily on the shore, and there was nothing else between us and the coast of Siberia.

Man's relations with the sea can be simply those of good neighbourliness, or they can be profound and subtle, almost mystical. Let us take a quick look at Italy and Japan from this point of view.

Italy, the greater part of whose perimeter is provided by the sea, stretches out into the Mediterranean like a great breakwater. Not for nothing did Arabian geographers call it 'Long Land'. But, looking at the life of the inhabitants with an ethnologist's dispassionate eye, it is hard to see that the sea means much to them.

Not many years ago the phrase 'maritime Italy' was in vogue. But this was less a true and accurate description than a slogan, an aim, an ambition, often frankly admitted to be such, the expression of a desire to re-establish a better relationship between a people and its geographical environment.

Most of our basic habits are tied to the European continent, not to the Mediterranean.

Our basic food (apart from flour products, vegetables and fruit) is meat, the products of stock-raising; fish and sea

* The name means 'recess under the bows' (of a Japanese ship), but its etymology is not clear.

products represent barely six per cent of the daily consumption of animal substances, measured in calories; and this percentage would no doubt be still lower but for the weekly religious restriction on the consumption of meat.

Our clothes, in common with those of the rest of Europe, are a characteristic heirloom of the barbarian invaders, who were continentals, horsemen and herdsmen. The ancient peoples of the Mediterranean (and their heirs, the Byzantines) wore draped clothing, but ours is sewn. Male dress consists essentially of tubes of material adhering closely to the body, as is suitable, and indeed necessary, for those who spend a great deal of time on horseback. Women's clothing consists essentially of infinite variations on the traditional Teutonic theme of blouse and skirt. Traces of a long past as nomads, horsemen and herdsmen are evident in the quantity of leather that we are in the habit of carrying about with us, in the form of shoes, belts, gloves, wallets, and purses.

Our houses are solidly built of stone or brick and squarely planted on mother earth; they derive from the north European and mediaeval fortress in which men barricaded themselves against storms and enemies. The popular attitude to water is generally fear, suspicion, and mistrust; only an infinitesimal proportion of Italians can swim. Our attitude towards the nude in life is entirely negative.

Since the Middle Ages all our mental links have led back to the European continent. The Sicilian Channel, or that of Otranto, can be crossed in a few hours in a small boat, but we have always regarded these narrow stretches of water as far more serious obstacles than the Alps, which are relatively impassable and are snowbound for a large part of the year. Tunis or Valona are much nearer Rome and southern Italy than Paris or Vienna, but how much more natural it seems to their inhabitants to go to the latter. If one turns on a wireless set in Bari or Palermo, it is generally easier to pick up Slav, Greek or Arab stations than those in northern Italy or France; but who does not tune in to the latter rather than to the former?

It is the land routes that unite us to the sister languages of the European family, to the sister provinces of European civilization, to Christianity, to the world of industry and finance of which we form part, to traditions of clothing and ways of life and patterns of behaviour and standards and outlooks that daily influence the society in which we live. The sea divides us from the Balkans and the Iberian peninsula, but above all it divides us from the Semitic languages, the sandy, torrid, and often strange and incomprehensible world of Islam. But for a few exceptions (Liguria, Naples, Venetia, and some stretches of the Adriatic coast and some islands), Italy has always been invaded and populated from its continental hinterland. Innumerable waves of men descended from the Alpine passes and through the gates of Friuli towards the cities rich with gold and marble, the fruit-laden trees, the southern sunshine and mild climate; and their advance continued until they were brought up by a final obstacle, the sea, a strange, mistrusted element representing another world.

In this respect no country presents a greater contrast than Japan. As soon as one acquires a little knowledge of the way the Japanese live, one is struck by the fact that this is a real maritime people, born and bred by the seashore if not in the sea itself. In Italy, when man reached the sea on the last stage of a long journey, he adapted himself as best he could to an unaccustomed way of life. In Japan, when he turned his back on the sea and finally went ashore, he got used to the new element reluctantly, and after two thousand years there is still something provisional about many aspects of his life on *terra firma*. For us the sea is basically an undependable element that surrounds and confines the land; the Japanese regard the land as a continuation of the sea—great waves that have solidified into islands. In both countries past ages have left deep roots which still influence the present and will certainly continue to do so for many future ages.

The Japanese diet is largely of marine origin. The staple food, apart from rice, vegetables and fruit, is not meat, but fish, which is the principal source of animal proteins. Every kind of sea-product is liked and sought out, from molluscs to seaweed, from shell-fish to sea-urchins. Fish is eaten in every conceivable manner—raw, roasted, boiled, fried, dried, powdered, diced, or in the form of paste. In some parts of the country even pork sometimes tastes of fish, because pigs are fattened on herring heads and tails. Until recent years animal products, the products of stock-raising, were entirely unknown. 'How disgusting to drink milk!' an old cook of mine once exclaimed when she brought my breakfast. 'How can the *danna-san* (gentleman) bear to drink this kind of cow's juice?'

The basic elements of Japanese clothing consist, in the case of men, of the *fundoshi*, a long narrow piece of white cloth that is wrapped round the waist and the lower part of the body; and in the case of women of the *koshi-maki*, a rectangular piece of cloth that is tied round the waist and descends nearly to the ankles. Nowadays the *fundoshi* and the *koshi-maki* serve as underclothes; they are covered by the kimono, which was imported from China towards the end of the first millennium A.D. But their ethnological significance remains unchanged and testifies to affiliations and connections with numerous peoples of south-east Asia and the Pacific. Both *fundoshi* and *koshi-maki* are obviously well adapted to a way of life that required frequent immersion and activities closely connected with the sea. Also the indifference to the nude in ordinary life which is so characteristic of the Japanese and of many Pacific peoples testifies to a long past lived on the seashore in hot climates.

The Japanese house—now acclaimed by architects as 'one of the most beautiful products of domestic architecture',* is a wooden structure pointing to life on coasts and islands. It stands on piles, which in the old days were high but have now been reduced to a few inches, and is built like a hull, a kind of immobile land-ship.

The visitor to Japan immediately notes the great familiarity

* E. A. Gutkind, *Revolution of Environment*, London, 1946.

with water displayed by everybody, men and women, old and young, rich and poor; the universal habit of the daily bath, which derives historically from Shinto purification rites; and the widespread ability to swim.

Finally, certain popular expressions are significant. With us cirrus clouds are commonly spoken of as being 'fleecy', with obvious reference to pastoral experience; in Japan they are called *uroko moyo* or 'fish-scale pattern'. And the Japanese equivalent of 'too many cooks spoil the broth' is 'too many sailors are pulling the boat uphill'.

# Children of the Sea

EVEN among the Japanese, of course, there are degrees of kinship with the sea. The closest to it of all, the true children of the sea, are in a category of their own. They are the Ama.

Who are the Ama, where do they live, and what do they do?

At numerous points along the coastline of the bigger and some of the smaller islands of Japan, there are villages where fisher-folk live who are distinguished from their neighbours by the fact that both men and women are skilled at every kind of fishing and underwater food-gathering. These are the Ama. Professor K. Yanagida mentions more than fifty villages in twenty-four different neighbourhoods where such underwater food-gatherers live.*

They live a life distinct from that of the ordinary Japanese, by whom they are considered rather as gipsies are with us, a strange people, possessing certain marginal skills, but rather crude and primitive. The word Ama is indicated in Japanese by two characters signifying sea-man or sea-women as the case may be, almost as if to suggest a relationship with fish, coral, and seaweed. It must never be overlooked, of course, that the Chinese characters used to indicate Japanese words often have nothing to do with their etymology, and this is no doubt a case in point, but the two ideograms certainly seem appropriate.

Nowadays nearly all the Ama men use the ordinary tools of their trade, that is to say, nets, lines, and pots; and many have good motor-boats and even sizeable fishing vessels. Their women do not dive for pearls, as is commonly believed,

* K. Yanagida, *Minzoku-gaku Ji-ten* ('Japanese Ethnographical Dictionary'), Tokyo, 1954.

but for edible seaweed and shell-fish (Plate 11). The men do not help them; that is left to boys.

No thorough sociological study of the Ama has yet been made, but the most superficial inquiry shows that they rarely marry outside their kind. In other words, they practice endogamy, an important factor in preserving their anthropological and cultural identity.

Nowadays they talk Japanese, using the dialects of the provinces in which they live. But I am assured that their vocabulary includes numerous words which are peculiar to them, and that their pronunciation sometimes differs from the usual, in short, that local people are definitely able to identify them by their speech. This might mean that they originally used a non-Japanese language of their own.

Like their neighbours, they are associated with various Buddhist or Shinto sects, depending on the province in which they live. In other words, there is no religious difference between them and their neighbours. It would therefore be interesting to make a thorough study of their folklore with a view to finding possible traces of a more ancient culture.

They have some interesting social peculiarities. Among other things, women seem to occupy a much more important position in the community and the family than is usual in Japan.

# On the Trail

FINDING the Ama—the real Ama—was no easy task.

One of the best-known groups of Ama women is that at Toba, not far from Nagoya in the province of Shima, where they work in the oyster farms founded by Kokichi Mikimoto, inventor of the method of producing pearls by cultivation. Every guide to Japan devotes pages of text and pictures to them, and many films have been made of them.

I had gone to see them a month previously. The weather was still bad for film-making. The period between the beginning of June and the middle of July or later is that of the Japanese rainy season, the form taken locally by the far vaster phenomenon of the monsoon, which affects the whole of eastern Asia from India to the Kuriles. The sea was rough and the water was therefore unclear, there was a continual drizzle from the low, grey sky, and the air was close and oppressive.

I was not very impressed by what I saw. The Ama girls of Toba had nothing in common with the mythological sea goddesses about whom some of my Japanese friends had talked to me; they were more like honest working girls employed at so much an hour to dive a few feet into the tranquil roadsteads of the Sea of Ise where the boxes containing the oysters lay. The whole atmosphere was of efficient industrial routine, which is an excellent thing in its place, of course, but differed greatly from the picture which had been planted in my mind by the possibly excessively romantic descriptions of my friends. Some of the girls actually worked exclusively for the benefit of tourists; a guide took visitors out in a boat to the place where they dived and, while they did so in bathing costumes reminiscent of those fashionable at Ostend or Viareggio fifty years ago, he explained to us the technical details of pearl culture, reeling off a patter in grotesque English which he had learnt by heart.

The real Ama diving girls dive for the delicacy known as *awabi*,* a kind of shell-fish, also known by its Spanish name of abalone, or for edible seaweed. But fishing up oysters and pearls is a prevalently modern development due to the ingenious Mikimoto. Toba, in short, was not the real thing, and there was no point in wasting time on it.

I went back to Tokyo and made more inquiries. A Japanese photographer, a friend of mine, suggested that I try Hatsushima, a small island seven miles out to sea from Atami, about seventy miles west of Tokyo; or Onjuku, a village on the south of the Boso peninsula, rather farther away on the other side of Tokyo. He was convinced that there I should find what I wanted; villages where the Ama still lived in the ancient fashion and did not work for tourists, but simply because that was how they had always lived.

I drove to Atami first.

The whole Japanese coast from the bay of Tokyo onwards is studded with celebrated holiday places and bathing and winter resorts. First of all there is Kamakura, a town rich in architectural monuments and memories of the period from the eleventh to the fourteenth centuries when it was the capital of the Shoguns, the hereditary military governors of Japan. Near it are Zushi, Enoshima and the many little villages of the Miura peninsula, hidden among pine-woods and rocky capes; and here, at Hayama, is the villa where the Emperor frequently retires to devote himself to the study of marine biology. Then comes the big curve of the Bay of Sagami, with the broad beaches of Fujisawa, Chigasaki, Hiratsuka, and Oiso. Then, after passing Odawara and some hills which descend to the sea in terraces planted with fruit-trees and rice, you come to Atami, where there are some of the most famous hot springs in Japan.

Exceptionally for the rainy season, the day was fine. As far

* *Haliotis striata L.*, and other varieties of the same species.

as Odawara the route followed the ancient Tokaido, the 'Eastern Seaway' which for nearly a thousand years has joined the two most important areas of Japan: the western area, which includes Kyoto, Nara and Osaka, and the eastern, the plain of Musashi and the great cities of Tokyo and Yokohama. Using the Tokaido is like travelling along certain Roman roads; every now and then the ancient track is visible, the new asphalt is overshadowed by ancient pines planted by the Shoguns, and every step recalls events, persons, usages of ancient times.

Before leaving I bought a cheap edition of the famous series of prints *The Fifty-three Stations of the Tokaido*, by Hiroshige (1797–1858), which were originally published at the beginning of last century. In the old days there were more than fifty-three post-stations where travellers could rest, change litters or horses, etc., along the three hundred miles that separate Tokyo (then called Yedo) and Kyoto. Hiroshige devoted a print to each station, recording with his superb draughtsmanship scenes from a life that now seems straight out of a fairy-tale—pilgrims going from shrine to shrine, the magnificent processions of the *daimyo* (feudal lords), the changing of horses or porters, the fording of rivers, rice fields covered with snow, rain on the bamboo trees, Mount Fuji, pine trees, the stormy sea, a horse fair, women tempting travellers in the evening in the taverns of Goyu. Some of the places are still identifiable, but Chevrolets, Buicks, Datsuns and Toyopets have eliminated the traces of horse-dealers and princes, poets and merchants, and the fifty-three stations of the Tokaido are now only names that you catch sight of out of the corner of your eye as you drive past.

I reached Atami in the evening. The hills were mysterious, undifferentiated violet masses descending into the sea and they were dotted about with lights of every colour. The sky was a dark blue transparency overhead and some stars had come out. A fine evening in Japan during the rainy season is a rare and magnificent thing. The air is soft and delicate, and lights are reflected and refracted with strange caprice.

Atami's wealth of hot springs is due to its situation on the edge of the crater of a huge extinct volcano. In the centre of the little town is a spring which is among the hottest that are known—about 210° F. It used to send up a great jet, or geyser, at regular intervals, but since the great earthquake which destroyed Tokyo and Yokohama in 1923 this phenomenon has ceased.

Every hotel and nearly every private house at Atami has its own hot spring baths. At one end of the scale these can be enjoyed in small private rooms in the luxury hotels, and at the other in the huge and stupendous establishments, reminiscent of the Baths of Caracalla, which are frequented by the masses.

In Japan, as is well known, it is usual for everybody to bathe naked at these hot springs—men, women and children together. To the western mind this is immediately suggestive, but nothing could be more mistaken. For one thing, nakedness is partially concealed by use of the small towel (*tenugui*) from which one must never be parted; and for another the behaviour of Japanese men and women towards each other is as decent as can possibly be imagined. It is all, of course, a matter of convention. In the Far East, for instance, up to the period of the first extensive contacts with the west, the human figure was always represented in art more or less clothed. Thus it can be said that in the east the nude is accepted in life but not in art, while in the west it is accepted in art but not in life.

At Atami I met a party of friends, Italian and Japanese, and next morning we left for Hatsushima in an infernally noisy motor-boat. We reached the island an hour and a half later. It is small, fairly flat, covered with vegetation, and consists of black or greyish volcanic rock.

A feature of Hatsushima is a peculiar social order which has prevailed there for several centuries and has repeatedly attracted the attention of sociologists. An archaic form of Communism prevails there. In some immemorial past, the island's elders decided that its resources were sufficient to support a maximum of about fifty families, or about three hundred and fifty people.

When this number was exceeded the young (younger brothers and sisters in particular) had to leave and earn their daily rice on the mainland. All the island's produce was divided among those who remained.

In practice the situation is rather more complicated. Property is jointly held, but the islanders are certainly not all workers; the system that prevails is more like a shareholders' co-operative. In some respects the system reminds one of the *maso chiuso* holdings in the South Tirol, where only the first-born inherits the shareholding. Most of the work, so far as I could judge, is done by casual labourers from the mainland.

One group of workers employed by these 'Communist' shareholders consists of about twenty Ama women and girls who gather seaweed and shell-fish off the island during the summer season. There is no real Ama village at Hatsushima, but only some long wooden huts where the women and girls are lodged during the working season. These huge and wretched dormitories reminded me of similar accommodation provided for girl rice-pickers in some places in upper Italy.

The Ama girls of Hatsushima were certainly more like the real thing than those who worked for Mr. Mikimoto at Toba, and the way they went about their work might well have been interesting. But all the other elements of Ama culture were lacking. There were no men or old women or children, there was no village, and all the curious and little-known aspects of the life of a completely maritime community were lacking.

So there was nothing for it but to try Onjuku.

There are three peninsulas within easy reach of Tokyo. The smallest is that of Miura, which we have already mentioned; the others are those of Izu and Boso. The Izu peninsula consists of mountains that plunge abruptly into the sea, forming innumerable promontories; it is covered with fabulous forests, is studded with hot springs and resorts, and is by far the most celebrated. But the Boso peninsula has its own beauties. The landscape of this quiet, rural region only a few miles from the capital is less dramatic. It consists of hills and valleys and small plains, and conceals a little world that seems to lie altogether outside time. Everywhere you come upon old Buddhist shrines and charming villas reflected in the paddy-fields; and customs survive here which have vanished elsewhere. In summer, for instance, you are quite likely to find children chasing dragon-flies and calling them by the names of the legendary heroes of the wars between the Taira and the Minamoto, which were fought eight centuries ago. When they catch a dragon-fly they believe themselves, in accordance with the pious Buddhist belief, to be holding in their hands the reincarnation of some ancient Samurai.

At Onjuku things turned out to be much better. There was a real *ama-buraku*, or Ama village, quite distinct from the other fishermen's or peasants' villages along the coast, from which it differed slightly in appearance. Here the Ama girls engage in their traditional calling of gathering *awabi* and edible seaweed. They do not wear the appalling white bathing-costumes inflicted on their colleagues at Toba by the management of the Mikimoto concern, but still dive in magnificent nudity, as they did when the painter Utamaro saw them two centuries ago.

The coast along the lower part of the Boso peninsula where Onjuku lies is very fine. Steep wooded hills plunge down into the Pacific, splitting up into capes and rocks, islets and promontories; and the projections enclose tiny bays and inlets, some narrow and constricted, almost like caves, others wider and less dramatic. The rocks consist of Tertiary sandstone lying in layers like piles of old books, and because of their brown colour, and the capricious abundance of vegetation that clings to them, the scenery could easily be grim and macabre. But, as the shore faces south and is flooded with sunlight, the effect is gay and fanciful. The impression created is that of a natural Baroque, similar to that of the Sorrento peninsula near Amalfi or Positano.

Many of the inlets on this indented coastline have small, quiet, white beaches on which the waves of the ocean beat. A number of them shelter little villages, some of which, like the seaside villages in parts of Liguria, have encroached on every inch of available space and sometimes even more. Houses cling to the rock wall, or are built like nests into natural caves and cavities. The fishing-boats are all well built and have modern engines, and are drawn up out of reach of the tide by ingenious hand-worked winches.

Immediately behind the cliffs are farms, rice fields, houses with big thatched roofs, and everything breathes a primordial peace and quiet, but down on the shore life is strangely restless. The roads climb and dip and twist and turn in crazy fashion, and plunge through narrow damp tunnels covered with aggressively green ferns. The people are hospitable, but have no time to waste. Business is concluded quickly, without protracted haggling. The sea, evil and fertile, rich in treasure but treacherous, will not wait.

The Ama village of Onjuku is situated in a wide, nearly flat opening on this coast. It consists of a number of simple, low, grey, wooden houses, arranged regularly along a few wide streets which slope gently down to the beach and the sea.

On the evening immediately after my arrival I watched the Ama girls returning from work in their boats. The day had been fine, but stormy clouds blew up and obscured the setting sun. The wind had churned up steep and angry little waves, and the women had put on their crude brown or blue kimonos, which they wore like togas. They flung them off to jump in the water and push their boats in, and their tanned bodies gleamed like gold in the warm sunset glow. If anyone had said that they had just been born of the sea, it would have been hard to contradict.

This promising opening was followed, however, by disappointment. I invited one of the village elders to the inn to discuss our film-making project. In Japan, of course, all approaches must be made in the correct hierarchical fashion;

a direct approach to the Ama girls would have been useless. He was a charming old gentleman with a face puckered into innumerable little wrinkles, but it was obvious that he was putting every obstacle in the way of our getting any real information about his womenfolk and their work.

'I'll send you two models tomorrow,' he said. 'They're very nice girls, and very pretty, they have worked for lots of photographers, and the rates are very reasonable.'

So that was that. Even Onjuku had become a show-place for tourists. We packed our bags and left.

I was at a loss where to turn next when I remembered Professor Tokutaro Yasuda. He would certainly be able to help.

Professor Yasuda is a Tokyo physician who has taken a lifelong interest in ethnology and anthropology. He has written many books, a number of which are well known; one of them,* on the origins of the Japanese people, has gone through I do not know how many editions. Like many scholars, he has his hobby-horse. This is his theory of the common origin of the Japanese and Lepcha peoples, based on their alleged resemblance in language, customs, and outlook. When one considers that the Lepchas live in remote and isolated Himalayan valleys in Nepal, Sikkim, and Bhutan, it is obvious that this theory makes heavy demands on one's imagination.

Professor Yasuda lives in a typical Japanese middle-class house near the residential quarter of Mita in Tokyo. The Japanese rightly scorn our barbarous habit of living in great concrete boxes divided up into compartments in which people live detesting, or at best ignoring, one another. They prefer living in houses of their own, and even in the heart of Tokyo the innumerable small villas surrounded by foliage of which the capital consists remind one of the country. They are nearly always built of timber, which in Japan is abundant and cheap, and their construction with solid cross-

* T. Yasuda, *Nipponjin no Kigen* ('The Origin of the Japanese'). Vol. II of *Ningen no Rekishi* ('The Story of Man'), Tokyo, 1954.

beams in the manner of a ship's hull gives them an internal stability which enables them admirably to resist the frequent earthquakes.

The professor's house naturally has a 'western room', a veritable chamber of horrors, with alabaster statuettes, velvet curtains, tassels, and Ingres's *La Source* hanging on a wall. Fortunately I was received in his Japanese-style study. Upon entering I had to remove my shoes before treading on the *tatami*, the rice-straw mats that cover the floor. The light of the sky, filtered through the foliage of a tree in the garden, flooded in through a big window. The floor was piled high with books in every conceivable language.

The professor assured me of the excellence of my idea of making a film of Ama life before it was submerged by the overriding spirit of commercialism. He is a little man, aged about fifty, with a very lively expression, and has the communicative nature of people who immediately take a lively interest in the work that anybody is doing. Japanese scholars sometimes enclose themselves in a kind of hieratic Confucian solemnity, and then they can be aloof and distant, but Yasuda was of an entirely different type. Every few minutes he jumped up to look for some book to illustrate a point he was making. Finally he produced a map of Japan he had marked with a lot of red-pencilled crosses along the coast.

'I don't know what to advise you,' he said. 'Those are the Ama colonies that still survive. But they have nearly all been spoilt by journalists, tourists and maniacs. At some places they ask for money before letting themselves be photographed, and at others they run away and hide.'

A woman came in and with great ceremony and many bows offered us tea.

'*O-cha do desu-ka*? (Would you like a cup of honourable tea?)' the professor asked.

'*Itadakimasu* (with pleasure),' I replied in the ritual manner.

The professor fetched an envelope full of photographs.

'Do you know where you might go?' he said. 'I've just had an idea. You must try the island of Hekura. I'm sure that

that's the place for you. There it is, north of the Noto peninsula, in the Sea of Japan. There you may still find the Ama in an unspoilt state. But you must be prepared for many difficulties. The reason why they are still so unspoilt there is that they don't want visitors and do everything they can to keep them away. You'll see that they'll do everything possible to deter you from going there; and if you go there all the same they'll do everything they can to put a spoke in your wheel.'

'Thank you very much for your advice, professor. Couldn't you write me a letter to someone in the island? Perhaps if they saw that I had an introduction to the *sensei* (professor) they might receive me better.'

'I'll write you a letter with pleasure, I'll do it straight away,' the professor said. 'But, as usual, there's only one real way of gaining the *entrée*.'

The professor looked at me with the eyes of a sage who can be very acute and practical when occasion requires; perhaps he was waiting for me to tell him that.

'You mean by giving presents?'

'Precisely. And they had better be generous, or you'll get nowhere at all.'

'What about a small wireless set, for instance?'

'Excellent. Or a watch would make an excellent impression too. But in any case you will have to be very patient and show an immense amount of good will. If you do so, I'm sure you'll be successful.'

We sipped more honourable tea, and the professor started asking me about my travels in Tibet and Sikkim with Professor Giuseppe Tucci. Inevitably we got round to the subject of the Lepchas. By the time I left it was dark, and I swear that I was almost converted to the illustrious scholar's theory of the common origin of the Lepchas and the Japanese.

## Pandering to Human Weaknesses

Soon after our arrival at Wajima a tall, listless, pensive-looking youth named Okizaki, the son of a local business man, called on us. Professor Yasuda had kindly written to him about us. Okizaki took us to a small and venerable hotel called the Fujiya ('the Fuji Arms'), where we were received with great cordiality by the landlord, the landlady, and the servants, who drew up kneeling at the entrance, in accordance with traditional usage.

Why is a Japanese hotel, particularly if it is a small, country one, always so much more inviting than a western hotel? It is difficult to say. Partly it may be because you are not received by a uniformed hall porter, often with a martial air, but by the women of the house or members of the proprietor's family. In a Japanese hotel there is no reception or inquiries or accounts desk, and no pigeon-holes for letters or counters divided off by glass partitions, and any suggestion of an office is absent; that sort of thing is relegated to somewhere behind the scenes. As soon as you enter you have to take off your shoes. You then make your way in slippers to a room where a waitress brings you tea and someone comes and discusses with you the details of the service that you require. You discuss your room, the probable length of your stay, the number and quality of the meals that you want, and all the details which will affect the size of the bill.

The ideogram for *yadoya* (hotel) is composed of elements indicating 'one hundred persons under a single roof', but in practice a Japanese hotel is like a private house. A western hotel is like a filing cabinet in which a lot of human beings are temporarily put away. Your first impression on entering a Japanese hotel is the home-like atmosphere, and your human weaknesses are subtly pandered to. A voice seems to whisper:

We know you are tired and nervy, and our only desire is to provide you with rest and refreshment. Here is a room that opens on to the garden, offering you green leaves and the sky for company. Soon your bath will be ready, and in the meantime we shall prepare your dinner and your bed for the night. *Anshin shite kudasai*, set your mind at ease.

We rested with a tranquil heart at the Fujiya. Actually it was a poor sort of place, but we were treated so hospitably that we did not have the heart to complain. That same evening we invited Okizaki to share our *sukiyaki*; *sukiyaki* is a characteristic Japanese dish consisting of meat cooked in soya sauce in a pan in the middle of the dining-table. We drank *saké* and sang very gaily. Okizaki kept reminding us not to allow our hearts to be tranquil about our prospects with the Ama. Foreigners had sometimes spent a day on Hekura, but staying there would be a different matter. He foresaw that the elders of the village would put innumerable obstacles in our way.

'They don't like outsiders to come and disturb the girls at work,' he said. 'The *awabi* season is short, and the girls' time is valuable. The best of them are capable of gathering £10 worth of *awabi* a day.'

The *jochu-san* (waitress), using wooden chopsticks with the usual dexterity, delicately laid the long thin slices of beef on top of the liquid in the pan. Every now and then she added onions, spices, sugar and strange, exotic vegetables. When the *sukiyaki* was ready we helped ourselves, using chopsticks to put the meat into a tiny cup containing the raw yolk of an egg; and we ate this delicacy to the accompaniment of white rice.

'And, apart from all that,' Okizaki went on, 'who knows what ideas the village elders will get into their heads? They'll be afraid of the girls getting swollen heads and demanding higher pay, or of their getting involved with strangers, or that the island will start getting flooded with tourists. They don't want their peaceful life to be disturbed. You'll see that they'll do everything they can to get rid of you and, if they can't get rid of you, they'll see that you're boycotted.'

Next day we spent in preparations. Okizaki advised us to buy rice, vegetables, *saké*, and presents to give away, and he got us *futon* (bedclothes), a *kaya* (net) to protect us against mosquitoes, and a lot of other minor essentials. He also found out that next day the Hekura-maru, a sixteen-ton fishing-boat, was leaving for the island, and he reserved places on board for us.

These preparations took us all over Wajima. It is a town of about 35,000 inhabitants, recently promoted to the rank of *shi* (township) from that of *machi* (village). Most of the houses are prettily arranged on the seashore at the foot of some hills. Wajima, like many Japanese townships, is also an agricultural and fishing centre. It is also well known for its lacquer work, an ancient industry predominantly in the hands of craftsmen.

The *ama-machi*, or Ama quarter, is separate from the rest of the township and lies where the low and sandy coastline meets the first rocks of a promontory. Naturally we went to see it, but what we saw did not reveal any conspicuous differences from the poor quarters of an ordinary Japanese town. In any case at this time of year, at the end of July, it was almost completely deserted. Most of the men and all the able-bodied women, besides a number of old women and children, had gone to Hekura for the *awabi* season.

In the old days the annual migration to the island took place in an impressive, ceremonial manner on a fixed date, the eighty-eighth day after *risshun*,* that is to say, at the beginning of May. Unless the weather were too bad, the bay of Wajima would be filled with beflagged boats, which at a signal from the *kucho* (head-man) raised their sails and set off for the island eighteen miles away to the west. The return journey took place on the two hundred and tenth day after *risshun*, that is to say on about September 10th, after the typhoon season had passed its peak. The return to Wajima

* *Risshun*, the first day of spring, occurs on about February 4th.

was also undertaken in common, and, according to the old people who remembered it, it was a highly colourful occasion. During the winter only cats and mice were left on Hekura.

Ama customs, were, however, revolutionized by the Second World War and the introduction of modern methods. Sailing boats have gone out of use, and nowadays the Ama all have excellent fishing vessels or motor-boats; and the trip to the island is no longer a hazardous enterprise to be undertaken jointly, but a four-hour trip that anybody can undertake at any time. Fishing for *iwashi* (sardines) has now assumed great importance, and occupies the men exclusively until June and beyond. The *awabi* for which the womenfolk dive are getting scarcer, and a number of families remain on the island all the year round. The annual migration still takes place, but not jointly and on a fixed date; it now takes place later in the year, in powered boats, and without ceremony.

*Rocks in the Seven Islands*

2. *The Ama children might have been born of the sea.*

3. *The village of Mikuria clings to a strange green rock.*

4. *The little harbour of Hekura; the Ama girls' boats can be seen at work offshore.*

7

8

5. *The busy scene on the beach at the end of the day's work.*

6. *Their mother and sisters are out fishing, and school is closed for the summer holidays.*

7, 8. *At the end of August the Ama and their womenfolk leave the sea and worship the gods; a big gilded palanquin is carried in procession round the island.*

9, 10. *Old Nakano prepares a reed boat on which the spirits of the dead will return to the sea after spending three days with their surviving relatives during the August festivities.*

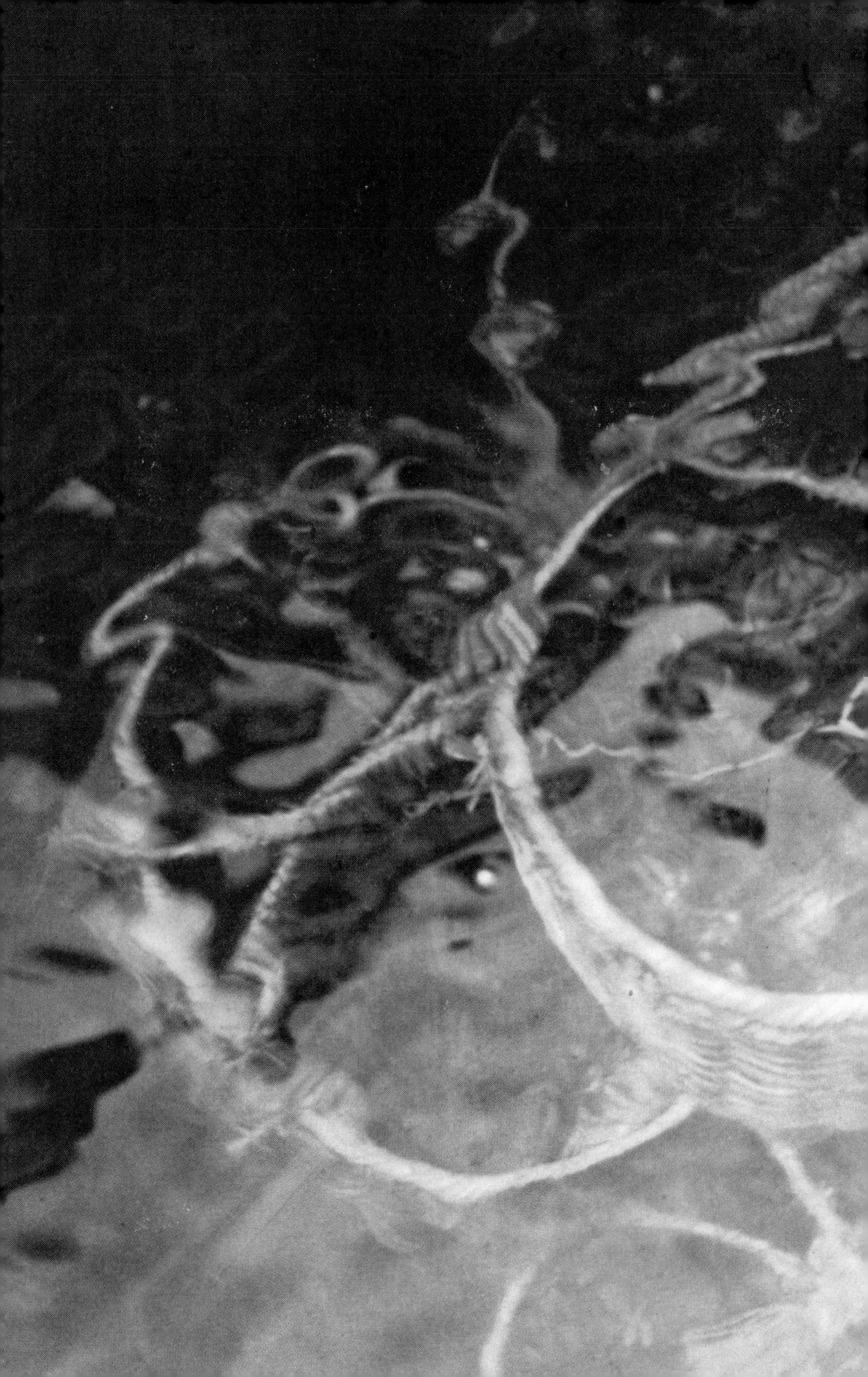

11. *Baskets full of* awabi *hung at the side of a fishing-boat waiting to be taken to market, at which they will fetch high prices.*

12. *The flying of these flags tells the world of a good day's fishing.*

# The Seven Islands

JAPAN is more Japanese by night than by day.

In the course of time some of the most characteristic features that impress themselves on the mind of the foreign visitor may fade from his mind—the sight of the delightful, almond-eyed children going gaily to school, for instance, or the country temples half-hidden among the cypresses, or the cherry blossom, or the waterfalls, or Mount Fuji, or the proud, contorted pine-trees along the rocky coast. But, when you have once heard the sounds of the Japanese night, they are impressed on your mind indelibly. There can be no forgetting the sound of the pipe of the *sobaya* (itinerant food vendor) wandering somewhere in the night, or the distant voice of a geisha entertaining a party and accompanying herself with the strange music of the *samisen*, a kind of lute; and finally there is the deep silence, broken only by the faint chirping of the crickets.

Later the dawn whitened the sky and we rose and took our bath. Immediately after our breakfast of seaweed, rice, fish, tomatoes, and *miso* (bean-paste) soup, a taxi arrived for us. It was impossible to cram all our luggage into it, and the overflow had to be accommodated in a small cart. At the entrance to the hotel the whole of the proprietor's family and staff gathered to bid us farewell with deep bows and choice Confucian compliments. Then, when the cab moved off, all of them, men and women alike, rose to their feet and gave us an enthusiastic, American-style send-off, with a great waving of arms.

The Hekura-maru, already packed with men, women and children, bales and bags and boxes of food, was waiting for us at the quayside. After we had managed to squeeze ourselves and our baggage on board there was not an inch of free space left. Our travelling companions were all from the locality—big powerful men with faces weather-beaten and tanned till they looked like old leather, women obviously capable of handling boats single-handed, and almost indecently healthy-looking girls. There were also three or four noisy and talkative young gentlemen equipped with cameras and straw hats, obviously on an outing from Kanazawa. They may have been admirable young men, but they could not stand comparison with the Homeric islanders all around them. Okizaki saw us off and recommended us to the skipper.

Finally a boy came running along with the mail, and the Hekura-maru's engine started up. We moved off, and a few minutes later passed beneath the little metal lighthouse at the end of the mole. The sea was calm, and the sun shone in a Mediterranean sky.

'And to think that in Tokyo it's almost certainly raining,' Murata remarked. 'How lucky they are in this part of Japan.'

In countries affected by the monsoon the weather behaves most perversely. Instead of the south winds that would be desirable and pleasant to mitigate the rigours of winter, the north wind prevails, making Japan, which lies on the latitude of Tunisia or Sicily, as cold as Austria or Transylvania. Instead of cooling breezes from the north to mitigate the heat of summer, hot winds laden with moisture blow in from the Pacific, covering nearly the whole archipelago with sticky heat. Not the whole of it, however; most of the rain falls on the southern coasts and the mountains that form the backbone of the main island; on the north coast and in a great part of Hokkaido the downpour is only sporadic. In these privileged places the sunshine is almost worthy of an Italian summer.

The monsoon is a vast phenomenon that affects a large part of Asia. The explanation is that Central Asia consists of great deserts that warm rapidly in summer and cool equally rapidly in autumn. In the winter great masses of cold air accumulate and contract over them, producing a high pressure zone, from which cold air then spreads out in all directions, resulting in the winds which blow regularly for many months from Central Asia to the east and south, towards India, Indo-China, North China and Japan, producing cold, clear weather. In summer the warming of the air over Central Asia makes it lighter and causes it to rise. As nature abhors a vacuum, air from elsewhere moves in to take its place, causing concentric winds to blow in towards the heart of the continent from the Indian and Pacific Oceans. These ocean winds are naturally heavily laden with moisture, which is precipitated on the land masses in their path, particularly the mountains. The result is the rainy season, so well known to visitors to south-east Asia, and the season of snowstorms in the Himalayas. The end of the process is marked in the Pacific by the fearful phenomenon of the typhoons at the beginning or middle of September.

While on the subject of the monsoon, it is interesting to note that this coast of Japan, where we were now enjoying the most brilliant sunshine imaginable, is covered in winter in deep snow. Because it faces north it receives the first precipitation of the winds from Siberia, the humidity of which is increased in crossing the Sea of Japan. Trewartha notes that 'this region is absolutely unique among countries with a sub-tropical climate. No other part of the world offers such a curious combination of tropical heat and humidity in the summer contrasting with a deep blanket of snow in winter.'* There are many valleys between Niigata and Kanazawa in which the snow reaches a depth of twelve or fifteen feet, incidentally making life very difficult for the inhabitants.

When we were some way out the sea grew very choppy. The young gentlemen from Kanazawa, though they paled and went green in the face, gave a splendid example of self-control, laughing and joking as usual. However, the sturdy young women who looked like the daughters of Neptune huddled pathetically at the bows. They kept going to the side

*G. T. Trewartha, *Japan: A Physical, Cultural and Regional Geography*, University of Wisconsin, 1945.

and leaning over, and they left a trail of undigested rice in our wake; which shows that one should never judge by appearances.

Soon we made out between one wave and the next Nanatsu-to, the Seven Islands, an archipelago of black or reddish, steep and sinister, volcanic rocks. Some of them looked like the heads of giants emerging from the sea covered with green hair—this was bamboo grass. We also saw pinnacles and natural arches rising from the sea; we should have liked to photograph them, but the little ship was now tossing so furiously that we did not dare let go and stand up to handle our cameras. On one of the islands, called Oshima ('Big Island'), there is a tiny village in which, I was told, thirty or forty Ama live. The big, strong girls who had been bringing their hearts up now gathered their remaining strength and got ready to disembark. The little ship took us to the lee of the island, where the sea was flat, almost like oil, and a big rowing-boat appeared and took off most of the passengers. The young gentlemen from Kanazawa disembarked too. They looked greener than ever, but they were still smiling, like good Samurai. Only a few passengers remained on board for the rest of the journey to Hekura.

Beyond the Seven Islands the wind dropped, and the waves, though still high, seemed not so steep; and it rained a little. At about twelve o'clock we made out the Hekura lighthouse less than a mile ahead.

The skipper told me that the island was so low that it was invisible until you were almost on top of it. He said that in the old days, before the lighthouse was built, it had been very difficult to find, particularly if a high sea were running; at any rate that was what the old people said.

A few minutes later the Hekura-maru entered the sheltered little harbour. It was surrounded by wooden houses, which had weathered to a fine greyish brown, which was sometimes almost pearly. The beach consisted of grey stones (Plate 5).

A small crowd was waiting on the quay. The men mostly wore white and the women were in short *yukata*, faded by sun and sea. More children of Neptune, companions and handmaidens of Ulysses. Strange to say, we and our mountain of baggage were totally ignored. Everybody obviously knew all about us already, because the Japanese bush telegraph works with lightning speed and efficiency. Was this reception a first polite hint of difficulties to come?

One thing, however, was certain. We had at last found the Ama in their natural state. This time we were in the presence of the real thing, not of a feeble survival overlaid by a strange and hostile world, as at Hatsushima or Onjuku.

Meanwhile a little man apparently aged about fifty (later we found out that he was seventy) silently approached us in

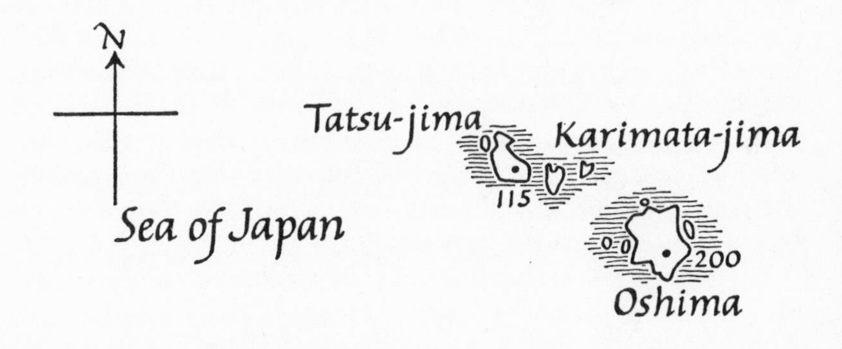


THE SEVEN ISLANDS

a boat, into which he put our baggage. Then he signalled to us to follow him in another boat, which was rowed by a half-naked, very serious-looking, young woman. We then went in procession to the Buddhist temple, which stands on a small eminence to the north of the main group of houses.

# Rock Raft

THE general shape of Hekura can be seen from the map overleaf. It is a very small island; a kind of raft built of solid rock which gives refuge for the night or during bad weather to about a thousand persons for a few months every year. Its maximum length is about a mile and its maximum width about half a mile. It is two and a half miles in circumference, and at its highest point reaches the giddy height of forty feet. Nearly in the centre of the island is a handsome stone lighthouse, with accommodation for the coastguards attached. The lighthouse was built in 1931. It is in wireless communication with the mainland, and private messages can be sent or received by courtesy of the coastguard services.

The island as a whole is flat. On the south-east, where the village lies, it slopes down gradually towards the sea, with long beaches of grey stones, but the north-western side, which faces the open sea, is rocky and steep.* There are numerous isolated rocks. The whole provides a vivid, varied, imaginative and impressive marine landscape, both above the surface of the water and below it.

Vegetation is scarce. Trees seem to have been indicated on the earliest maps, but no trace of them is left; all that remain are clumps of bushes, a great many reeds, *sasa* (bamboo grass), and horribly prickly briar. Here and there one or two small fields are sown in a makeshift manner with sweet potatoes. A glance at them is sufficient to reveal the spirit of the Ama, who are children of the sea and live on land as if in exile, only provisionally, so to speak. Cultivating the soil is obviously regarded as an inferior occupation, and only a few crones and youngsters engage in it. These people's whole life is centred on the sea.

* Plates 14, 15, 39, 41, 63.

ISLE OF HEKURA

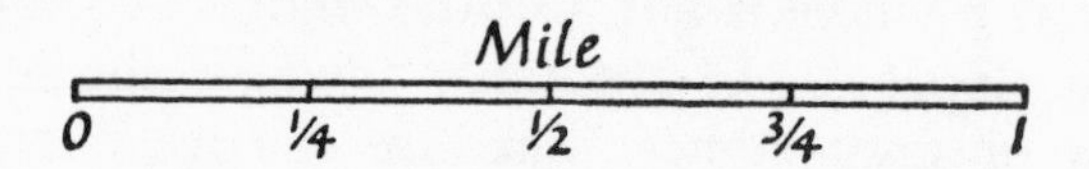


Names of parts of the village of Hekura

| | |
|---|---|
| 1 Nakakita | 6 Demura |
| 2 Kamikita | 7 Onishi |
| 3 Homura | 8 Kaminishi |
| 4 Benten | 9 Sangenya |
| 5 Koiwa | 10 Owada |

The island is of volcanic origin; the rock—mostly black, but always dark—of which it consists is Andesite. I was able to observe a few slight volcanic phenomena at a depth of from thirty to sixty feet off the north-west coast, where gas bubbles emerge similar to those off the coast of Vulcano in the Aeolian Isles.

One curiosity is a small lake called the Dragon Lake, which has led to a strange legend and cult that I shall mention later. The whole island is notably rich in subterranean springs which provide water sufficient for the Ama's needs. A slight sulphurous smell emanates from some of the rock pools, the temperature of which is perhaps slightly above the average.

A characteristic of the animal life of Hekura is the number of cats. They are half wild, and are left on the island when the Ama return to the mainland. Presumably they survive by foraging for mice. The island also has some non-poisonous snakes. Swallows and gulls abound. A point important to visitors is that mosquitoes are numerous and voracious. Specimens of a rare species of snail (*Hekura maimai*) are occasionally to be found.

The village is composed of about three hundred houses strung out along the shore. At one time the village consisted merely of hutments used during the summer months only, but since 1935 more substantial buildings have gradually been put up, and now, particularly in the centre of the village and facing the harbour where the better-off families live, there are real houses fit for habitation throughout the year. Electric light was installed in 1954. Hekura now forms part of the local government district of Wajima. A Buddhist priest, a schoolmaster, and sometimes also a policeman and a doctor, are resident there during the summer.

## Divine Patronage

IT is interesting to note that Hekura also has a population of gods. The human inhabitants who enjoy their patronage and protection all live on the low side which faces the mainland and receives the first rays of the morning sun; the gods mostly live in proud solitude on the opposite side, each on his own promontory, with his own little chapel, reinforced to protect it against the sea.

If we make an imaginary tour of the island following the coastline on the map, near its southern tip we first find a temple dedicated to Okutsu Hime ('the Princess of the Hidden Bay'), a poetical celestial personage associated with ancient sea legends. On the rocks of the uninhabited shore we come next to the temples of Gion, Kompira, Kwannon and Ebisu, between which lies the little Dragon Lake, the water of which looks green enough to serve as a magic potion. On the inhabited shore there is the Buddhist temple of Hozo ('the Treasure of the Scriptures'), a shrine dedicated to Ryu-Jin, (the Dragon of the Green Lake), the shrine of Benten, as well as numerous other shrines, statues, steles, and stones, all of which are objects of veneration of various kinds. Men and gods are thus close neighbours, and the seen and the unseen are in constant communion.

It is worthy of note that for more than fifteen centuries two profoundly different religions have cohabited in Japan—Shinto, the original religion of the Japanese, a primitive, poetic, nature and ancestor cult, and Buddhism, the great universal religion introduced from the Asian mainland in the sixth century A.D. It is as if with us the paganism of the classical world had not been completely submerged by Christianity, but had managed to survive side by side with it, maintaining its own identity and independence through the centuries.

At times Shinto and Buddhism have been in conflict, but on the whole they have cohabited peacefully. Indeed, they have blended to such an extent that in the eyes of most Japanese they are not conflicting faiths, but merely different aspects of the same reality. At a more sophisticated level, the great Buddhist missionary Kobo-Daishi proclaimed in the ninth century that the *kami* (the Shinto gods) were simply manifestations of the Buddha. At the level of everyday life, Japanese families are nearly always associated both with a Shinto shrine and a Buddhist temple. Recourse is had to each for different purposes. Marriages and 'presentations' of the new-born are nearly always celebrated in the Shinto *jinja*; funeral services nearly always take place in the Buddhist *tera*.

At the peasant and fisherman level Japanese religion is a blend of primitive magic, ancient myths, local cults, and a number of more specifically Buddhist beliefs concerning the impermanence of all things, the transmigration of souls, and the sanctifying virtues of love and piety. All the deities that share the restricted living-space of the island with its human inhabitants are essentially protective.

At Hekura the shrines of the Princess of the Hidden Bay, Gion (which recalls a famous shrine at Kyoto), Kompira, Ebisu and that on the Dragon Lake, as well as those dedicated to Ryu-Jin and Benten, are Shinto; the small shrine of Kwannon and the temple of Hozo are Buddhist.

The cults of Kompira, Ebisu and Benten are characteristic of Japanese fisher-folk, though they are not confined to them.

Kompira is an extremely popular deity, about whom the chroniclers have little to relate; and that little is doubtful and conflicting, as is the case with us in regard to a number of saints who are surrounded with an odour of legend and remote antiquity; sometimes, apart from pious traditions, all that is really known about them is their names. It is typical that in the figure of Kompira (who for centuries has been identified with Susa-no-wo, 'the Impetuous Male', brother of the sun goddess Amaterasu, the supreme figure in the

Japanese Elysium), Shinto myths are blended with others of Buddhist origin; in the latter Kompira appears as a kind of virile, war-like aspect of the Buddha, a kind of Archangel Michael who combats heretics and enemies of the faith. However that may be, Kompira is considered the patron of travellers and seamen, and shrines and small temples are dedicated to him in many parts of Japan, all connected with the celebrated shrine of Kotohira on the island of Shikoku.

Ebisu is a deity of obscure origin. He is one of the Seven Spirits of Good Fortune who appear so frequently in the Japanese minor arts. The are generally represented on board a ship heavily laden with bounty of all sorts, and are to be seen painted on silk or carved in ivory, or modelled in earthenware, porcelain, or metals of various kinds. As for the name of Ebisu, it is no doubt significant that *emi* or *ebi* means 'smile'. He is the patron of honest labour and trade. He is represented as a princeling in ancient Japanese costume in the act of catching with rod and line a fine fat pink dentex (*tai*). Japanese shopkeepers often display him in their premises side by side with another member of the seven, Daikoku, the spirit of wealth, who is represented with two sacks of rice. Popular imagination has added to these two figures a mouse happily nibbling away at the grains of rice pouring through a hole in the sack under the sacred personages' very nose.

The great national festival of Ebisu takes place on October 10th. There is a curiosity attached to this. There used to be a popular belief that in October all the Japanese gods assembled at the great temple of Izumo on the Sea of Japan. Hence at Izumo this month came to be known as *kami-ari-tsuki* (the month of the gods), while in the rest of Japan it was called *kami-na-tsuki* (the month without gods). Ebisu, being slightly deaf, according to popular belief, failed to hear the summons to join his colleagues at Izumo, and therefore remained in his own shrine, where he could be worshipped accordingly. It is recorded that in the old days on the annual festival of Ebisu innumerable processions from the eight hundred and eight streets of Tokyo (then called Yedo) converged on the great shrine of Ueno in a fantasmagoria of lights, dancing and song.

Benten, a goddess, is another of the Seven Spirits of Good Fortune. She is represented as a charming and beautiful princess in ancient costume, often carrying a musical instrument because she is considered a patron of the arts. Sometimes she appears riding a dragon, and in many places obscure links with archaic snake cults appear to survive in her. She has been called the Japanese Venus, but the resemblance is entirely superficial. She could equally well be called the Japanese Minerva, with whom she also has attributes in common, for she has wisdom and eloquence in her gift. The sites dedicated to her are nearly always on islands, and her little shrine at Hekura, as can be seen from the map, is situated on a rock near the harbour—on an island off an island.

The word 'shrine' may suggest to the reader a kind of chapel complete with altar and sacred image. In the case of the Shinto shrines this would be quite wrong. The Shinto gods are rarely represented and, when they are, their image does not stand on the altar but elsewhere in the sacred building. The focal point of the cult is the *shintai*, the 'body of the god', generally a polished metal mirror concealed in a small wooden ark. It is the *shintai*, representing the divine presence, which on festival days is carried in procession in a heavy carved and gilded wooden palanquin. Buddhist temples and shrines, however, bear a great resemblance to Roman Catholic places of worship; they are equipped with altar, sacred images, candles, and rosaries, and incense is used and they always contain flowers as a symbol of divine love.

The cult of the Dragon of the Lake and of the Princess of the Remote Bay are, so far as I could establish, entirely local.

Coming to the Buddhist places of worship, the Kwannon-do, or 'Hall of Kwannon', is no more than a small chapel surrounded by a high stone wall to protect it against the fierce northern gales. Inside there is an image of Kwannon, who is one of the most popular Buddhist deities, and in some respects can be compared to the Virgin Mary. She stands for divine love and compassion, and recourse is had to her in times of danger, grief and suffering. But there are also profound differences, indicating two fundamentally different attitudes to life and the supernatural. The west, which invented science, tends to precision. The Virgin Mary is a human being with a definite, specific position in the world's history who by special grace became involved in the supreme cosmic drama. Orientals prefer to see things through symbols and allusions, keeping details vague and everything tinged with mystery. Kwannon is a symbol of goodness, compassion, and divine love, but physically nothing more than a mental prop, in some ways rather like the dove of the Holy Ghost.

Her cult was born in India. Kwannon was originally a male deity known as Avalokitesvara ('The Lord who Looks Down with Compassion') who in the course of centuries underwent great and sometimes astonishing transformations. In Tibet he became Chen-re-zi ('He with the Compassionate Eyes') and is incarnated in the Dalai Lama. In China, where his name was changed to Kuan-yin, as a consequence of a process difficult to follow he gradually changed sex and the divine compassion became infused with a subtle feminine warmth.

The cult of Kwannon is one of the most widespread in all the northern Buddhist countries.

The chief temple of the island—in some ways fulfilling the role of its parish church—belongs to the Jodo sect. This is an extremely simple and popular form of religion founded by the Japanese monk Honen (1133–1212). According to Honen, all human beings are capable of escaping from the cycle of rebirth and of ascending after death to the 'paradise of pure earth'. To secure this release neither meditation nor fasting are required; nor is it necessary to submit to arduous discipline or carry out good works; all that is needed is total and absolute faith. The Jodo sect has a big following, particularly among the less educated classes in Japan. Jodo priests marry.

Nowadays, in a spirit of emulation of the activities of the Christian missions, it engages zealously in social and charitable work.

# The Face of Him Who Knows Nothing

As soon as we arrived in the island we settled down for a stay that might be long or short, depending on circumstances. At last we had found some real Ama, and we had no intention of leaving without making our film.

Thanks to Okizaki, we were allowed to stay in two first-floor rooms in the temple building, where we assembled our numerous belongings, arranged our beds (the men in one room and Penny in the other), and put up our mosquito nets. The temple consisted of a central hall covering an area of about thirty *tatami*;* it was here that the altar stood and the people gathered for services and on festival days. The priest and his family were accommodated next to the big hall. All the rooms—for eating, sleeping, meditating, praying, or meeting for ceremonial purposes—were irregularly but well arranged and were contained in what from the outside might slightly cynically be described as a big grey wooden hut. The only exterior decoration was a small porch leading to a small concrete space on which it was pleasant to walk barefoot.

In Japan, generally speaking, the attitude to the sacred is less solemn than it is with us. When no inn or other accommodation is available in a Japanese village it is the normal thing to be accommodated in a Buddhist temple where all the activities of everyday life, dressing, eating, resting, working, and, in the case of children, playing, take place with the greatest possible naturalness. The sharp distinction between the sacred and the profane is a western cultural characteristic; in the Far East the divine is diffused everywhere, so to

* The *tatami* is the rectangular rice straw mat used as floor-covering in Japanese houses. It represents the area necessary for a man to lie down in. At Kyoto and in the Kwansai the measurements are 77½ by 37 inches and in the rest of Japan 71½ by 37 inches.

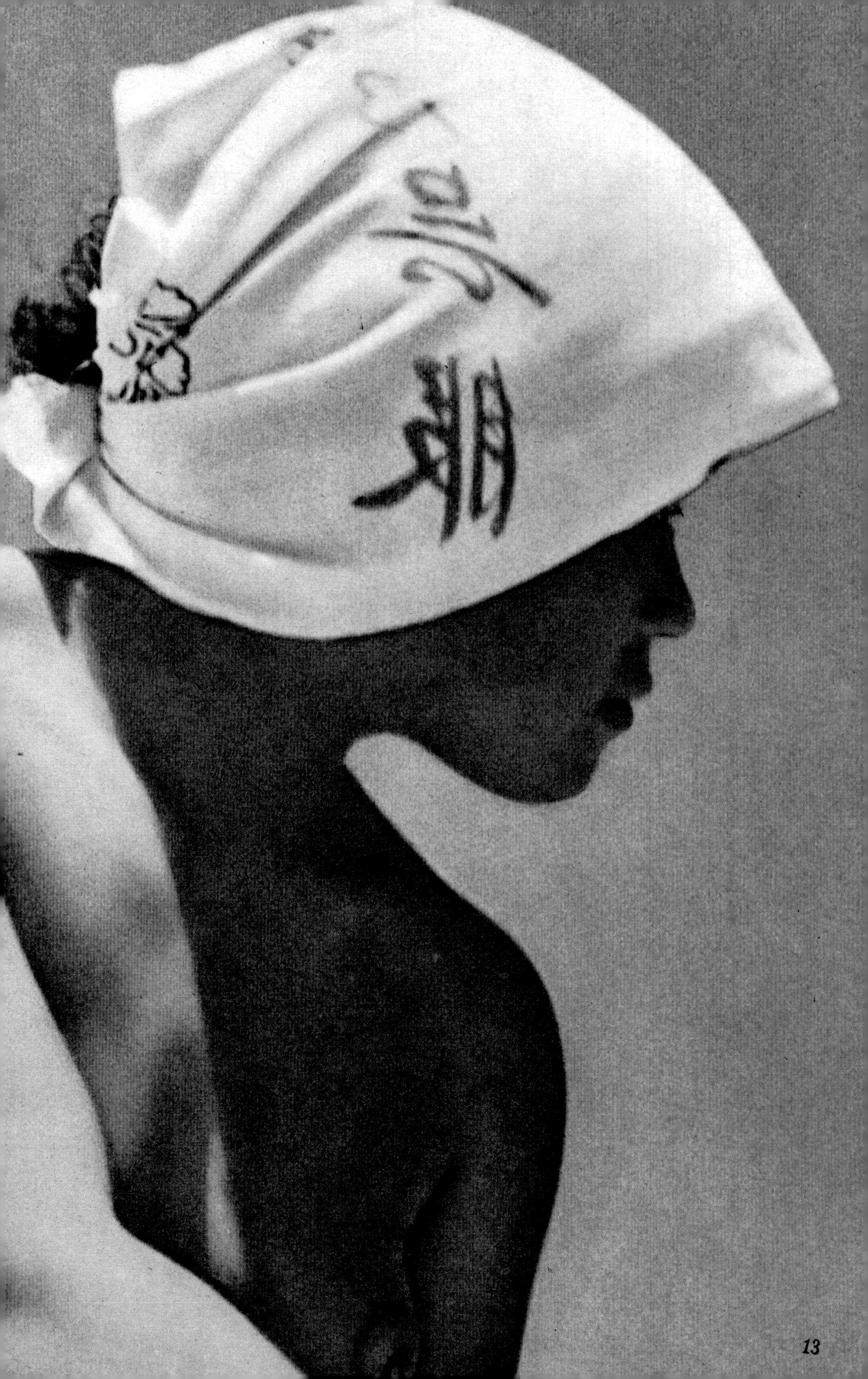

14. *The northern shore of Hekura consists of iron-grey rocks.*

15. *The inhabitants live on the stony south-west beaches.*

16. *The houses are built of wood and the roofs are weighed down with stones to prevent their being carried away by the gales.*

17. *Ama discovery of the harpoon-gun.*

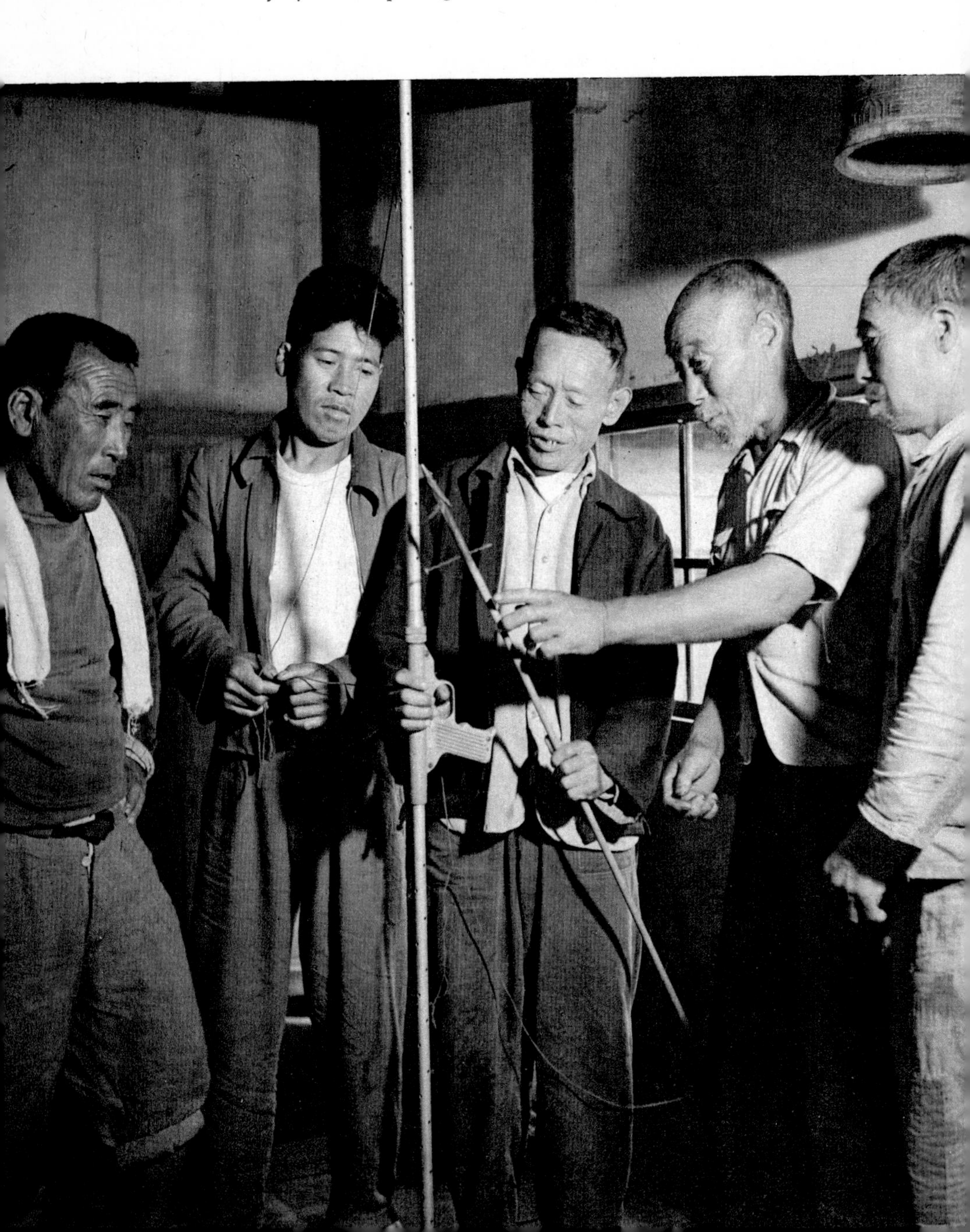

18. *Gossip round the brazier in the evening.*

19. *Edible seaweed ready to be packed and sent to market.*

20. *Silvery* awabi *shells.*

21. *Dawn of a festival day; the* torii *- ancient sacred gateway of the Shinto cult - is decorated with ropes and tufts of rice straw.*

22. *Ama children help their elders to pull out the big palanquin for the annual festival.*

23. *The priest of the island's Buddhist temple in his ceremonial robes.*

24, 25. *Evening in the priest's house; his wife, the school mistress, corrects her pupils' exercises while he writes sacred formulae on a white kimono.*

26. *Offerings and coloured paper lanterns on the family altar in an Ama house.*

27. *Lanterns lit for the festival in honour of the Princess of the Hidden Bay, a maritime goddess worshipped in the island.*

28. *Shinto ceremony outside the Shrine of the Divine Dragon.*

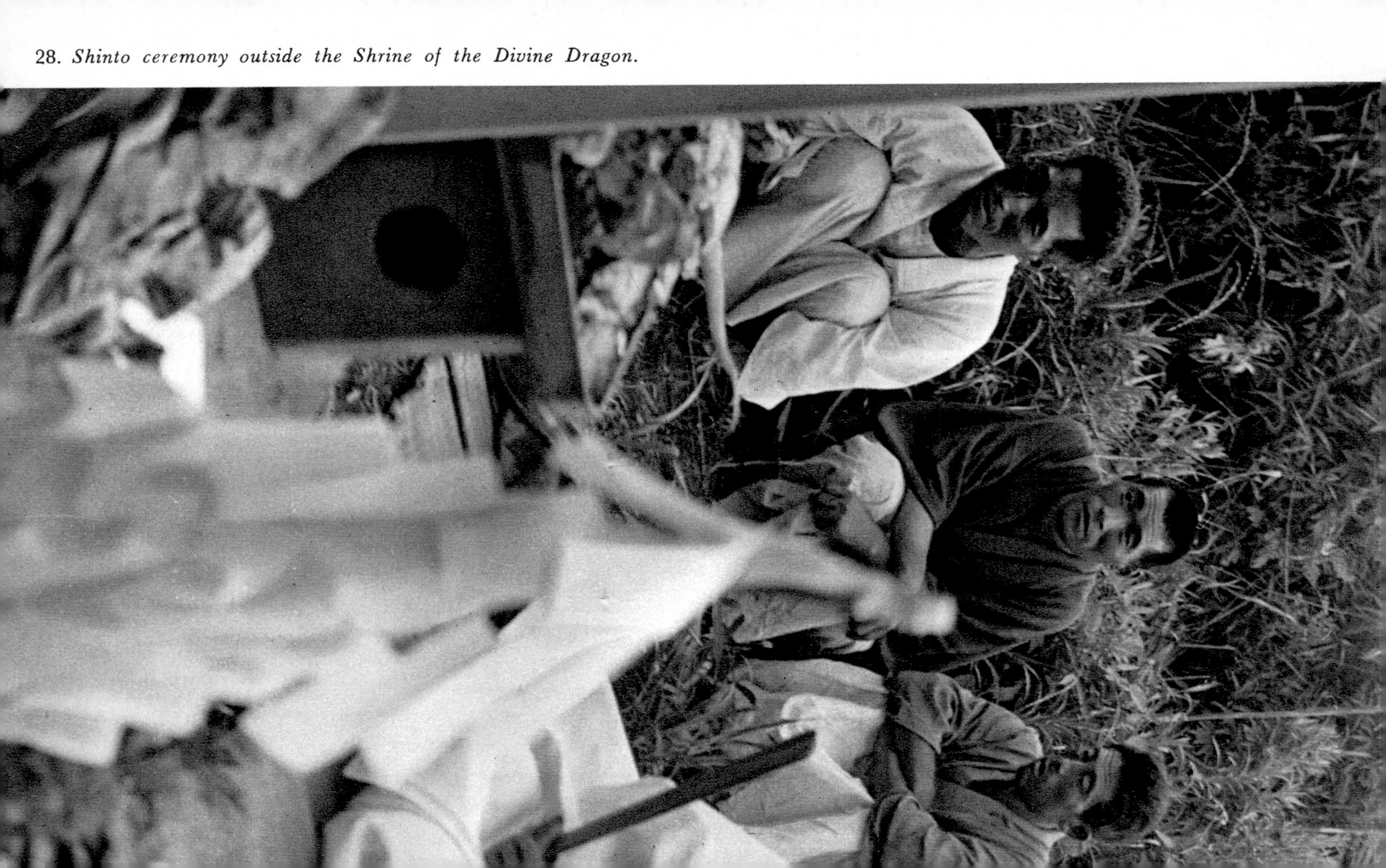

29. *The Shinto priest of Hekura.*

30, 31, 32. *The festival continues until late at night with drink, music and song.*

33, 34. *During the day-time only children are left in Hekura.*

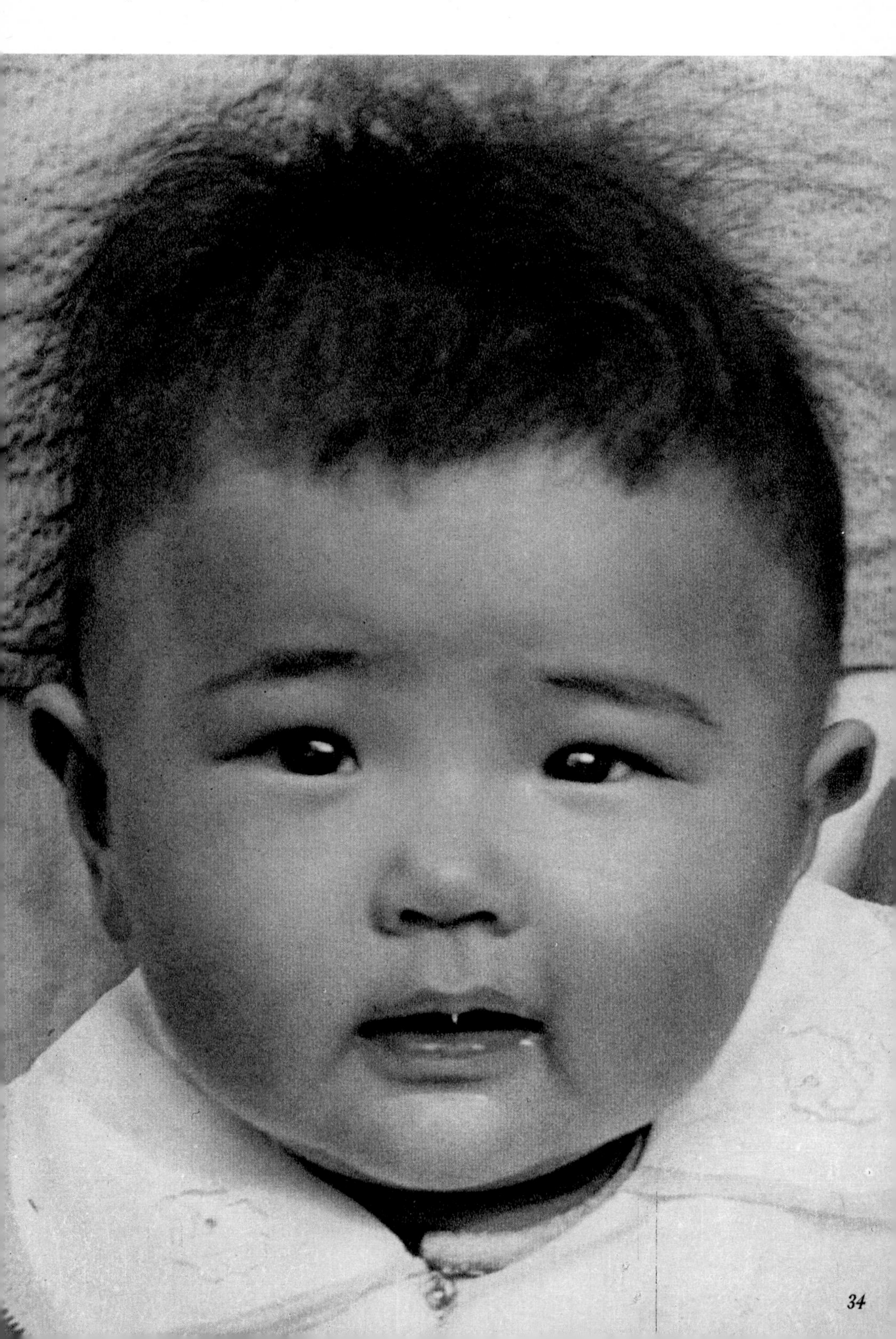

35, 36. *The Ama women are good mothers as well as skilled divers.*

37. *Clothes are worn for festival day at Hekura.*

38. *The sun is up and the Ama get ready for the day's work.*

39. *When the sea is too rough to go out in boats the Ama women seek out a spot on the sheltered side of the island for their work; if there is an east wind they have to climb down the cliffs on the northern shore.*

40. *The diving girls' working equipment consists of* nawa (*rope*), te

*l tool for detaching* awabi *from the rocks*), *and* oke (*wooden tubs*).

41. *If the sea is too rough there is nothing for it but to go back to the village.*

42. *Brother and sister go to work a mile offshore, where the biggest* awabi *are to be found on the seabed.*

43. *When the crew consists of girls only, the strongest girl handles the single scull.*

44. *Getting the rope ready before diving.*

45. *These goggles are worn under water.*

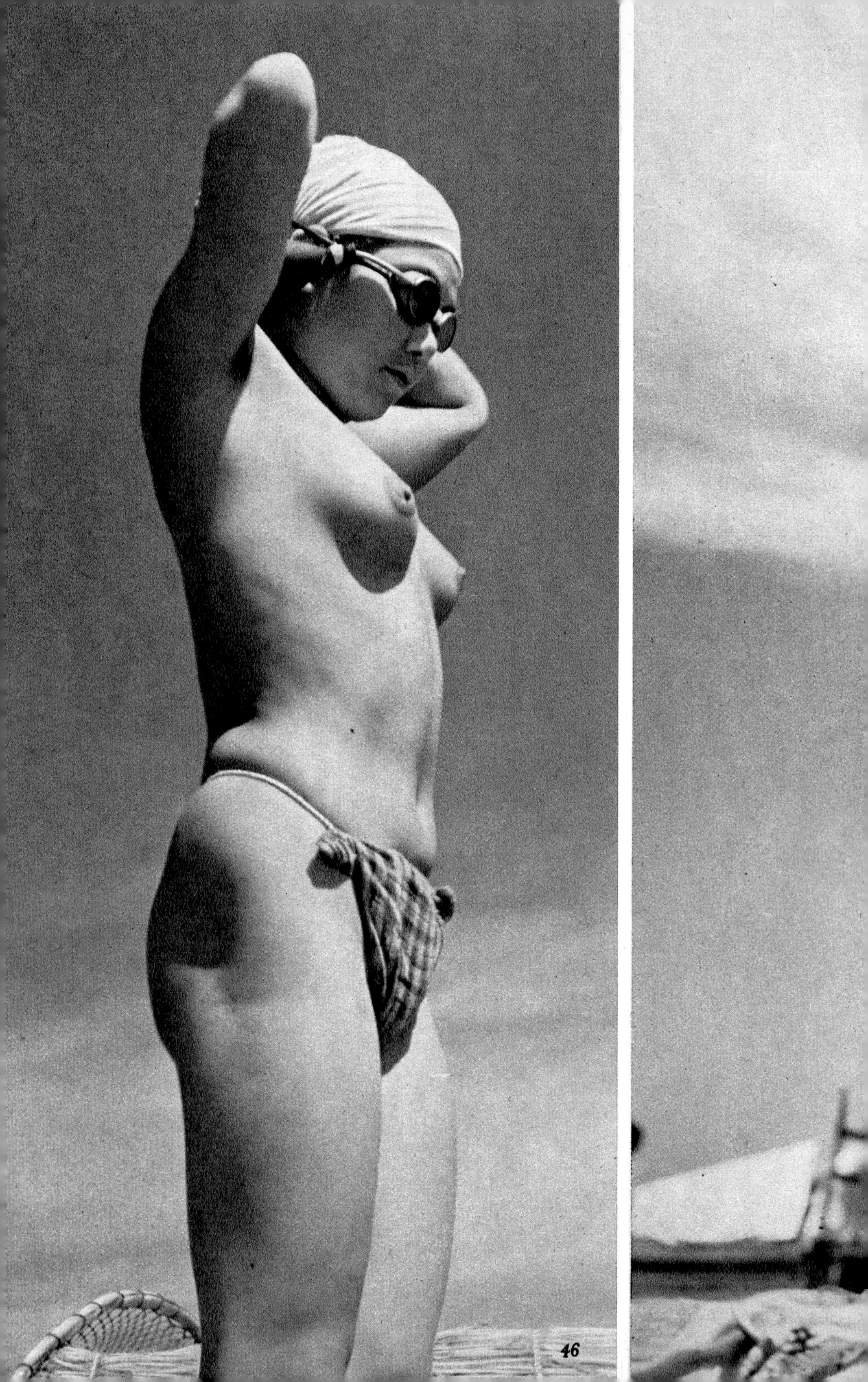

48. *Diving girl armed with her* tegane.

49. *The diving girls' goggles are provided with rubber bulbs which equalise the air pressure on the eyes in deep water.*

50. *Some girls use the headpiece familiar in Europe.*

51. *Bound for the sea-bed.*

55. *Hanging on to the side of the boat for a breather between dives.*

56. *On the way up to the surface.*

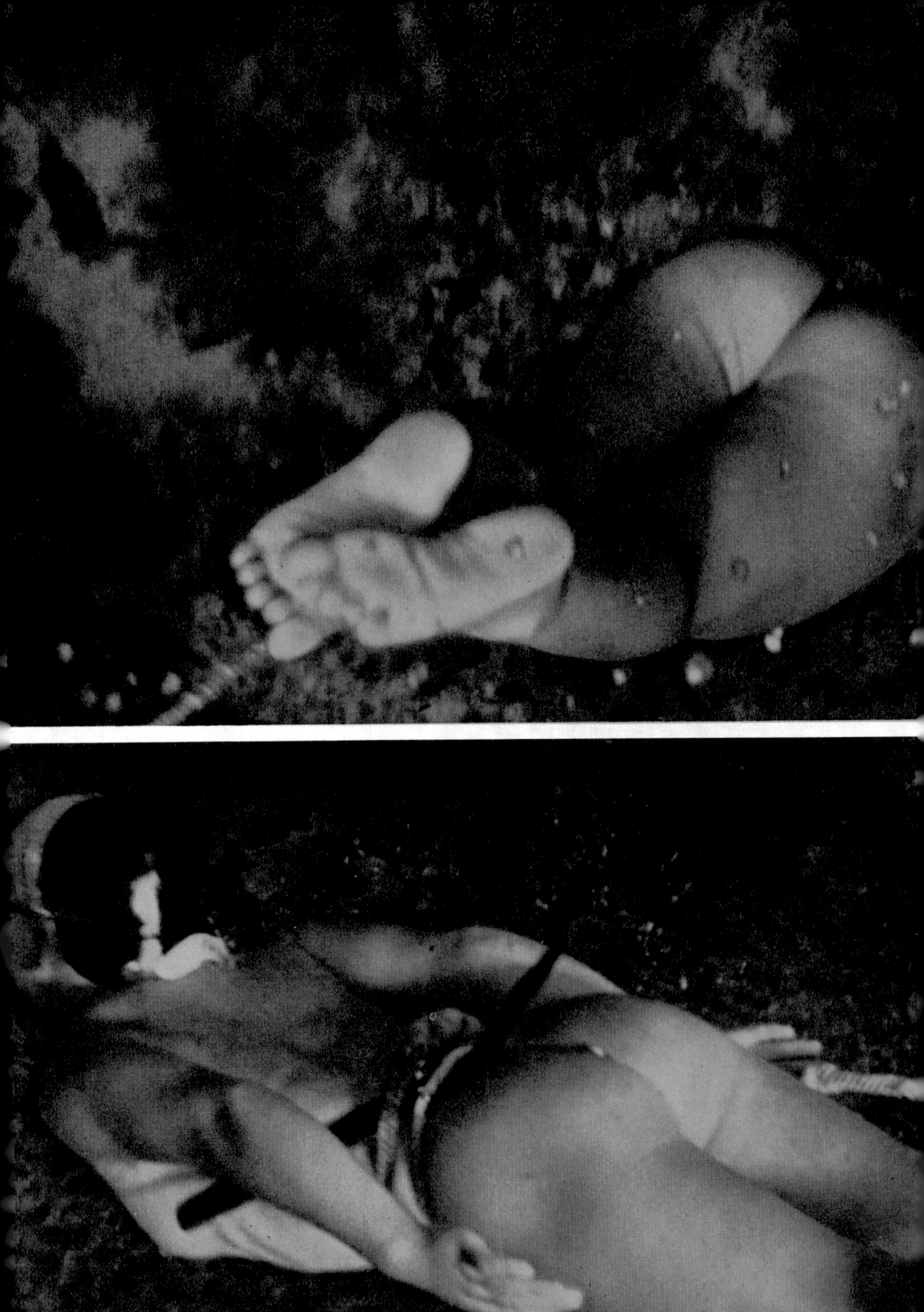

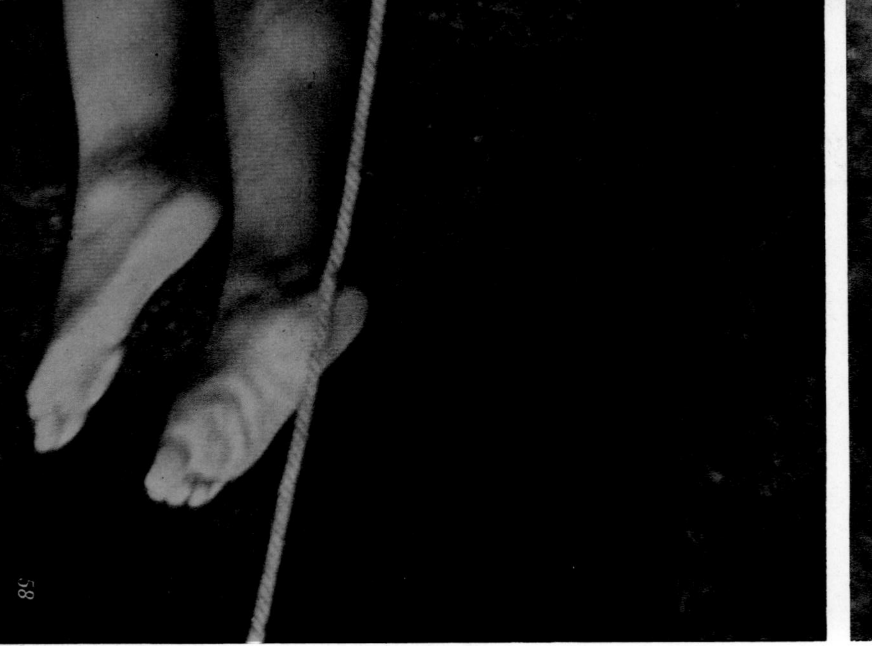

57, 58. *The most skilled divers are older women who have had plenty of experience.*
*Some dive for* awabi *to depths of sixty feet and more.*

59. *They begin diving at the age of about sixteen and go on until past the age of forty.*

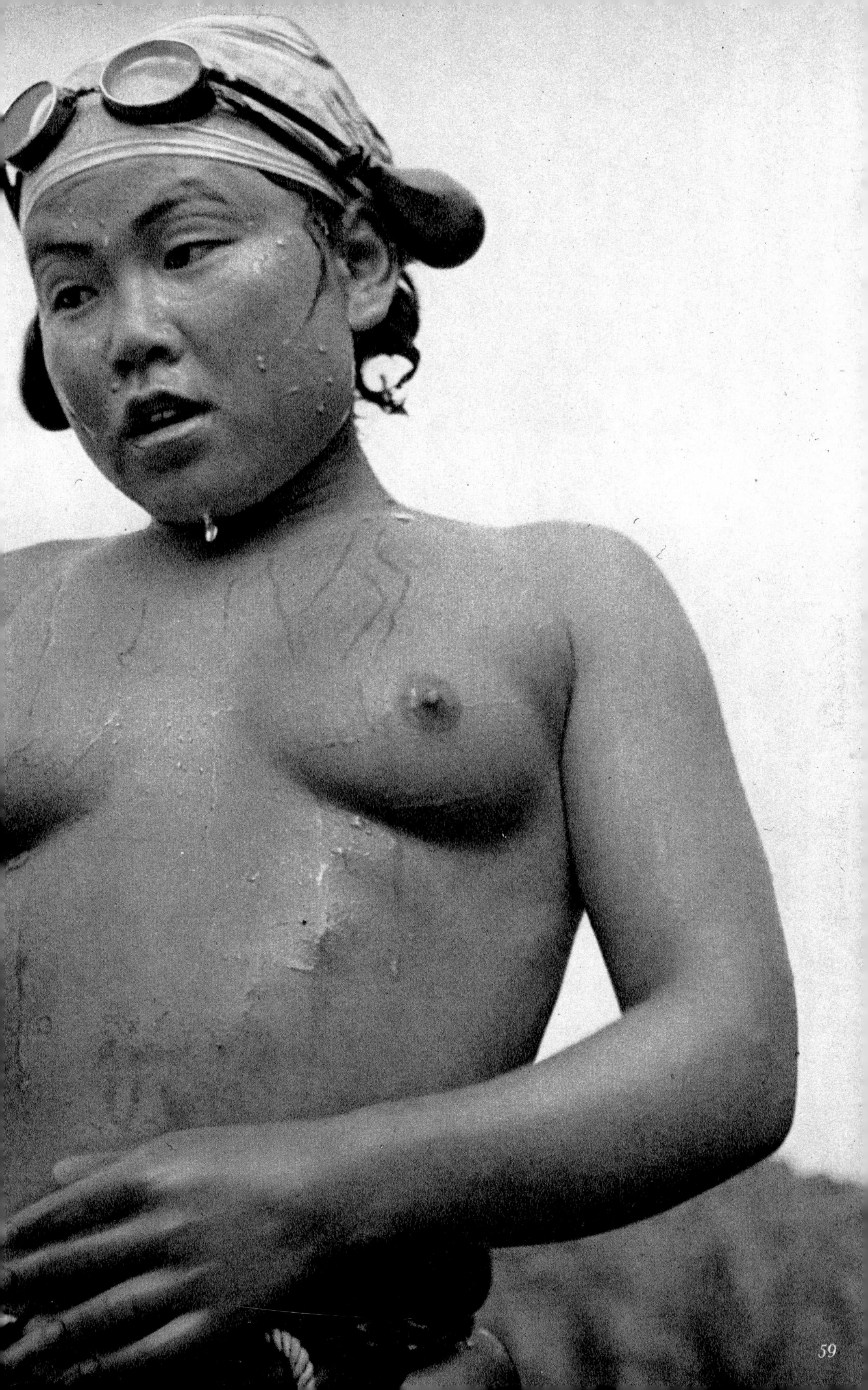

60. *The bucket of fresh water.*

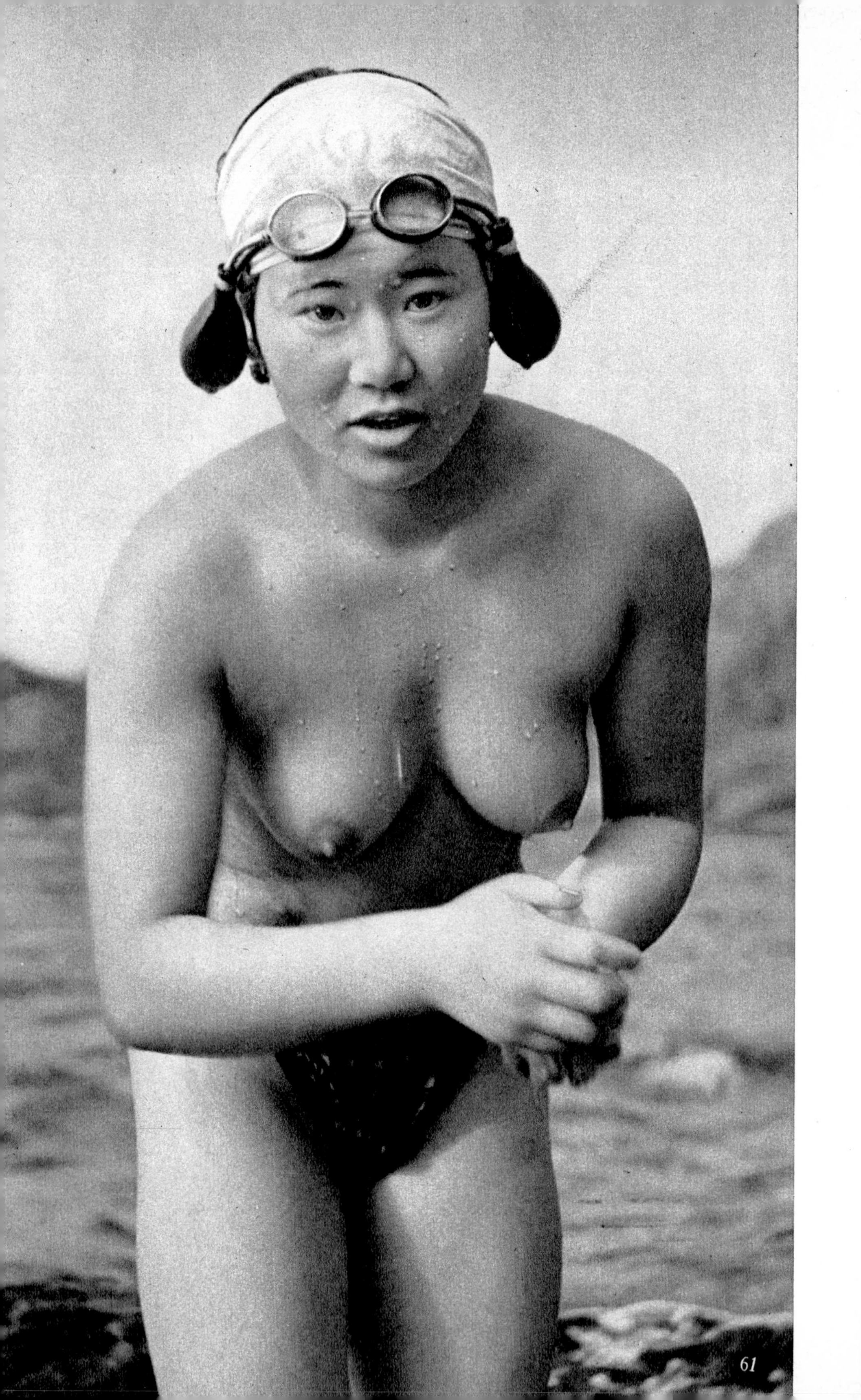

speak, rather like an electrical current of low voltage, silent, continuous, and ubiquitous.

We settled down very comfortably in the temple. The smell of brine and seaweed entered with the fresh breeze through the big windows; the *tatami*, though old, were clean; and the washing facilities, as always in Japan, were ample. In addition to a proper bath with hot water all day long, there was a pool of fresh water in the little garden only a few steps from the kitchen. Mr. Takada, the priest,* received us very hospitably. He was a bespectacled young man of quiet and studious appearance, and had qualified as an elementary schoolteacher before becoming a priest. His wife, a charming and reserved little woman, was also a qualified teacher, and she was helped in her household chores by an Ama girl who for health reasons was not allowed to remain for long in the water. The priest and his wife had a baby a few months old.

When we arrived a party of older boys and girls in charge of a schoolmaster were also staying at the temple. They all had geologists' hammers, specimens, butterfly nets, and preserving boxes, to say nothing of little notebooks filled with vertical notes and pencilled sketches. They spent their time engaging in little scientific expeditions among the rocks. The passion for science shown by Japanese of all classes and ages is striking and extraordinary, and it is not difficult to trace the roots of this well known characteristic of Japanese civilization. Such things as classifying the wings of obscure insects, spending whole afternoons noting the movements of birds and fish, or tracing the history of an ancient geological upheaval in a cave, represent the adapted, up-to-date form taken by the traditional Japanese religious love of nature and the traditional and very much alive Japanese sense of the immanent. Unfortunately we had no opportunity of getting to know these young people and their master better, because they left next morning, loaded with dried seaweed, beetles in bottles, and fragments of the island rock, smiling and gesticulating in a ballet of greetings, smiles and bows.

* Plate 23.

As soon as we were alone we started exploring the island, hoping in the process to find some way of breaking down the barrier that the inhabitants were trying to erect between us and them. To describe their attitude as hostile would be an exaggeration; they merely displayed a studied indifference to our persons and our possessions. The Japanese have an insatiable curiosity about everything new, strange, or unaccustomed, and no very great knowledge of their character was required to enable one to conclude that this attitude must have been imposed by the village elders. This was another aspect of the Japanese character, which from time immemorial has been accustomed to discipline and, if necessary, dissimulation. What the islanders showed us was *shiran-kao*, 'the face of him who knows nothing', to use a common Japanese expression.

On the first day we had the bad idea of appearing with our cameras; it was sufficient to look through the view-finder to cause everyone in sight, men, women, and children, discreetly to disappear, leaving the landscape empty. For the next few days we scrupulously concealed everything having a view-finder or a lens. We should obviously have to find some other approach to these people, requiring more time and patience.

Fortunately the island was fascinating in every respect. In the first place there was the silence, and the open and unlimited horizon; you breathed sky, space, and solitude, and men lived here as they did for ages without being deafened and enslaved by their own marvellous and disastrous inventions. There were no motor-vehicles, no loudspeakers, no made-up roads. The mainland was less than twenty miles away to the south, and in the clear morning light you could make out the mountains of the Noto peninsula. Nevertheless, here you seemed out of the world, in a land of myth and dream.

From the temple a path of flat grey stones* led with many ups and down in the direction of the north-east tip of the

* Plate 15.

island, to a rock called Taka-dokoro ('The High Place'), where the shrine of Ebisu stood. Except for the last stretch, the path was flanked by wooden houses;* and here the Ama led their cheerful, noisy and tranquil lives between kitchen, bed, boat, nets, and water. Their life was completely amphibious. Even the youngest children left their mothers' arms to climb about in the boats and play in the waves near the shore, while older children romped about farther out and men, tanned by wind and water till they looked like rusty nails or bundles of muscle and sinew, repaired nets or caulked their boats, and magnificent, nearly nude young women returned from their diving with boxes full of *awabi*.

I thought of the fishing villages in Sicily, where I lived for a long time after the war, and the contrast could hardly have been greater. The attitude to the sea in the two places was almost opposite. In Sicily the men spent a large part of their working lives in boats without ever acquiring true familiarity with the sea, often without even learning to swim, and the women, dressed in black, remained shut up in their houses. The sea was regarded as a dangerous and hateful monster, a penance to be borne because it could not be avoided, and the fisherman's life was regarded as the hardest and cruellest of human conditions.

Men delude themselves that they look at life with their own eyes, that they are individuals who form their own independent judgments and opinions; in reality their judgments and opinions are formed for them by the culture in which they are born and brought up. There is no reason why the men, women, and children of Porticello, Sferracavallo and Cefalù should not live in a state of familiarity and intimacy with the sea similar to that of the Ama. But the history, the cultural formation, of the two groups differ, and what may seem possible in theory is impossible in practice.

Leading from the temple in the opposite direction, towards the south-west corner of the island and the Okutsu-hime Jinja, was another path of flat, grey stones (very hot to one's

* Plate 16.

bare feet), twisting and turning and rising and falling following the broken line of the shore and separating the houses from the water. Here too the sons and daughters of the sea spent their daily lives between their houses and the waves; and here the life was more intense, as the districts of Koiwa ('Little Rocks'), Demura ('Harbour'), Onishi ('Great West'), and Kaminishi ('Upper West'), form the heart of the village. Here were the few offices and shops, as well as the homes of the more important Ama families, those of old Shirosaki, for instance, the head of the fishermen's co-operative and definitely the most important man in the island. The coastguard and lighthouse offices, the doctor's consulting room, and the school lie a little apart.

The school, as always in Japan, is a handsome building with ample playgrounds. Even in the most remote and inaccessible and poorest parts of Japan two things always strike the stranger: there is never a house without a bath and never a village without a school. A dirty Japanese is highly exceptional, and so is an illiterate Japanese; the latter in spite of the fact that, what with *kana*, numbers, and *kanji*, being able to read and write requires a knowledge of more than fifteen hundred characters. Outside the Hekura school there is a statue of Ninomiya Kinjiro, represented as a boy of about twelve carrying a heavy load of wood on his back and reading a book. Kinjiro was a famous teacher and man of letters of the Tokugawa period,* a man of humble origin who, being unable to go to school, educated himself while working in the mountain forests.†

Beyond Kaminishi one comes to Sangenya ('The Three Houses'), followed by the big curve of Owada ('the Bay'), where the village straggles to an end among reeds and low walls in the direction of the *torii* of the Shinto shrine of Okutsu Hime. This is where the poorest families live, and the boats drawn up on the shore are less handsome.

In Hekura, as everywhere in Japan, where sleeping late is

*1600–1868.

† Ninomiya Kinjiro was born in 1787 and died in 1856.

regarded as effeminate and reprehensible, life begins early in the morning; in Japan, which is, of course, traditionally the country of the rising sun, nobody admires the sunset, which stands for death and decay; and the moment when the sun first peeps over the horizon is regarded as the most auspicious as well as the most beautiful of the day. This, incidentally, is another example that goes to show how all our actions, attitudes and beliefs are cultural in origin, arising out of the culture in which we live. There is no such thing as natural man; there is only cultural man. But let us return to Hekura. While the first rays of the sun are still making a playful pattern of light and shade among the beach stones outside the houses, *amado* and *shoji* (doors and windows) are opened, the women go to the wells to draw water, the men appear, stretching and drying themselves with towels, to the accompaniment of animal-like grunts and exclamations. In their very first actions of the day the Ama men and women give vent with immense satisfaction to their primitive vitality, their health, their *joie de vivre*. Voices rise all along the shore, exchanging greetings, comments on the state of the sea and the wind, joking and leg-pulling.

Then comes breakfast of rice and sea food; and then, between half past seven and eight, preparations for the day's work begin. Ropes, tackle, anchors, oars, and boxes are taken on board the boats, and children too small to be left alone are often taken too. The whole area between the houses and the shore is filled with bustling activity, and boys and girls noisily help their elders. Someone starts up the engine of his boat and leaves, towing seven or eight rowing-boats behind him. The diving girls are ready for their long day's work. If it is cool, they wear crude cotton kimonos; if it is warm, they wear only the triangular cotton slip that they jokingly call *kuro-neko* or 'black cat'.

Unless there is a sudden change of weather, the village is practically deserted all day long while the boats with the women and some of the men on board are out at the fishing grounds which stretch a good way round the island to a depth of between twenty-five and fifty feet. That leaves the children (Plates 2, 6), who during the holidays spend the whole day playing in the water, the few men who are not fishermen, the coastguards and lighthouse keepers, one or two shopkeepers, a few old men, and a lot of old women. These last are the most extraordinary old women in the world. Having spent their whole lives on or in the sea, they are unable to remain idle now that they are restricted to the land. Bent and shrivelled and burnt up by the sun, they tirelessly climb half-naked from rock to rock, searching dark cracks and hollows and pools known only to themselves for crabs or fish or a handful of seaweed. Sometimes they are accompanied by a small boy or some little girls, and then they give instruction to their charges and impart to them the secrets of the sea. If the Ama young suggest spontaneous generation from the waves, the old women suggest final dissolution into the same element.

At about five o'clock the Ama girls' boats return from their fishing grounds, alone, or in groups, or in line ahead. The harbour and all the inlets on the eastern side of the island begin to fill with people, voices and smoke;* the children run to meet their mothers and big sisters returning from their day at sea with boxes full of *awabi*.

The warm evening sun gilds their bronzed flesh. After coming ashore many of them pour buckets of fresh water over themselves to remove the brine from their hair and skin.† The tackle is taken indoors, the boats are pulled up on the beach, the boxes of *awabi* are left to be taken away by the men from the co-operative, and a clerk notes down the share of the catch to be attributed to each family.

Evening falls quickly over the island. The Ama eat before dark. By the time night has fallen only a few tremulous little lights remain burning for a short time in one or two kitchens. Then everyone goes to sleep.

* Plate 5.
† Plate 60.

# Uncrowned King of Hekura

We spent the first few days finding our way about. We wanted to see how the Ama lived, and to consider how best to film their mythological way of life; and we hoped that they would gradually get sufficiently used to our presence to come forward and volunteer their help. But progress, at any rate so far as the second part of the programme was concerned, was exceedingly slow.

Fortunately we were very comfortable at the *tera* (temple). The day began with a magnificent meal from the depths of the sea. Instead of bread and coffee and other agricultural and continental products we ate strange little molluscs and shell-fish, seaweed salads, crustaceans that had been dipped in boiling water, and a slice of dentex, the whole supplemented by rice and bean soup. Our palates and digestion quickly adapted themselves to this totally unaccustomed diet; it was tasty, nourishing, and digestible. Lunch and dinner consisted of the same theme with minor variations.

After a short time at Hekura we felt ourselves turning into Tritons and syrens; we almost found ourselves touching our skins to make sure we were not growing scales. The sea was everywhere and in everything, in the air, in our food, in our talk, and in our thoughts.

During the day we wandered about, stopping occasionally to exchange a few words with the ageless old women, the amphibious children, the hirsute men who laughed like cavemen must have laughed after a successful mammoth hunt. For the time being it was better not to approach the Ama girls. We had come across parties of them lying on the beaches on the deserted side of the island, warming themselves round a fire after their work, but their behaviour was not very polite or friendly. Whenever we spoke to them they gathered into little groups and started tittering, hiding their faces behind their hands.

We did not go about in groups, of course. I generally had Penny with me; it was easier to strike up a conversation if I was accompanied by a woman, even though she was a foreigner. Mr. Murata, who was highly skilled at solving ordinary problems, very soon became discouraged and wanted to throw his hand in, and it was easy to see that at heart he disapproved of the whole business. He could not understand why a foreigner insisted on wasting his time and money among these uncouth sea-folk who were no credit to his country while there were so many marvels of nature and art in the rest of Japan. Takahashi was very young and totally inexperienced; he was eager to make himself useful, but the accumulation of novel circumstances was too much for him. The boat frightened him ('at last an example of a non-maritime Japanese', Penny remarked), the women made him blush, and the men filled him with alarm.

In conversation the islanders showed the usual lively Japanese curiosity about everything concerning our families, the country we came from, our eating and sleeping habits, our entertainments, and the education of our children, but not one of them ever asked what we were doing in these parts. They obviously knew perfectly well, but as usual wanted to avoid awkward and embarrassing questions. Their nearest approach to the subject was to inquire how long we intended to stay.

When we arrived, Shirosaki-san, the head of the fishermen's co-operative and the uncrowned king of Hekura, was away on a fishing trip, but as soon as he returned we went to see him.

He lived, as I have mentioned, in the Demura quarter opposite the harbour, where the more important families live. His house, built entirely of wood, was raised on piles somewhat higher than those usual in Japanese houses. The interior was divided up into a number of areas all more or less open and leading into one another, and in the middle of the biggest was a square pit, the hearth (*irori*), indicating that it was the kitchen. It was a simple house, frugally furnished, but not poor. The framework consisted of strong timber darkened by time and smoke; the panels that formed the walls and ceiling, and the furniture, were perfectly functional; there was nothing superfluous, but the essentials were of excellent quality.

We were received by Shirosaki-san himself, a man of seventy who looked little more than fifty. He was tall and broad-shouldered, disliked circumlocution, and went straight to the point.

'*Yoshi*, welcome, make yourselves comfortable. Eh, Shizu, bring the honourable tea.'

We squatted by the hearth. The honourable tea was brought by Shirosaki-san's two granddaughters—tall, assured, silent, earthenware-coloured, diving girls in their twenties, bare-breasted like goddesses.

'What on earth brought you to these remote parts?' he went on. 'Hekura is nothing but a deserted rock, with absolutely nothing of interest to offer.'

'On the contrary, Shirosaki-san, you are quite wrong. After living in a city for many months one wants to come to a place like this, it is a pleasure. What do you do when you want a change? You go to Kanazawa or Niigata or even to Osaka, don't you? When we want a change we come to Hekura.'

'Also you must be very uncomfortable at the temple. I know how you foreigners live. You can't possibly like our food. *Sashimi* (raw fish) revolts you, doesn't it?'

'Not at all, we've got used to it. We're perfectly happy at the temple.'

'In any case the Ama girls are very busy just now, and they must not be distracted from their work. We're at the height of the season; it only lasts three months.'

'I haven't said anything about the Ama girls, and I know it's the middle of the season.'

'*Yoshi*, *yoshi*, that's all right, then. Obviously I was under a misapprehension.'

We had the same conversation, with variations, a number of times, not only with Shirosaki, but with his son Iwai-san, an oriental Ulysses aged about forty, a magnificent specimen worthy to be sent to other planets as a representative of the human race—virile, tanned, handsome, and completely unaware of the fact, strong, self-assured, and serene.

Appearances, however, were deceptive, and perhaps Iwai-san was aware of it; in fact he generally kept silent. His magnificent physique and his head worthy of Neptune concealed a mediocre mind and an indecisive character. He was completely under the thumb, not only of his formidable father (that was intelligible enough), but of his mother and his daughters too.

However, a very unfavourable comparison to him and the whole Shirosaki family was provided by some semi-human, semi-civilized, semi-townsmen who came from the mainland to do business of some sort with the old man. 'White bodies and flat souls', Penny exclaimed when she saw them. They regarded themselves as persons of importance because they wore glasses and handled leather purses and papers instead of oars or marine engines. They spoke to us from time to time in appalling English and made comments such as: 'These wretches don't even have *tatami* (mats) in their houses. You should come to Kanazawa and see what fine hotels and cinemas there are there!'

# Key to the Ama's Hearts

The days passed, and the situation remained unchanged. We found no way of making a breach in the barrier of polite aloofness erected against us by the Ama and their womenfolk.

The weather varied. Sometimes it was magnificent in the morning, and then became overcast and dull, and the sea turned from brilliant blue to iron grey; sometimes it was greenish like a lake. When the sun shone it was warm, but when the wind blew cloud in from the open sea it was often quite chilly.

One afternoon I decided to do some underwater fishing with a harpoon gun on the deserted side of the island, where the cliffs plunged steeply into the sea. Penny came with me, and waited for me on a headland from which there was a fine view. When we set out the weather was fine, but during the short walk across the island, and while I was putting on my flippers and cleaning my headpiece, the sky became overcast, everything grew gloomy, and a cold wind blew up and made the sea quite choppy. However, after all these preparations I went in.

As soon as I had done so I was delighted that I had not changed my mind. How magnificent was this submarine world to which I had penetrated. Once more I thought with gratitude of the inventor of that simple and revolutionary device, the snorkel, which has revealed to us a whole new dimension of nature, hitherto invisible and inaccessible, though so easily within our reach. It is indeed a simple device, nothing but a rubber tube and headpiece and a bit of glass, but it breaks down the barrier of the surface of the sea and takes you into a new world; it is rather like taking a plunge out of space and time.

In geological times the fury that shook the island caused avalanches of huge rocks to pour down the whole length of it that faces the open sea, forming precipices, caverns, and arches and creating this fantastic and uncanny landscape, the features of which were abrupt gulfs, pinnacles and chasms and huge rocks piled higgledy-piggledy on top of one another, all fading rapidly from view in the strange, greeny-blue submarine opacity and distorted and magnified by submarine optical effects.

The waves went on beating against the black rocks. From below they provided a silvery ceiling in a state of perpetual violent agitation, full of whirling eddies of bright, scurrying bubbles. The movement of the water caused the long leaves of the seaweed to wave in passive helplessness, and tiny, purple fish floated this way and that as the water moved them. This dark, cold abyss was vaguely frightening. Everything all about was severe, primordial, inhuman.

Swimming was very tiring, mostly because little ripples kept filling the tube with water and cutting off one's breathing, but actually it was less difficult than might appear. I looked up, and saw Penny waving to me to come back. I waved to her, hoping she would not be too impatient, because I was delighted with this austere submarine world, and wanted to remain in it until I grew too cold.

Moreover, I had spotted a dentex; it seemed a big one, and had been swimming about at medium depth, as they generally do inshore. It had of course spotted me too, and it spent a long time looking at me, without taking to flight; it merely retreated to a safe distance with a flick of its tail. I followed it cautiously to avoid frightening it and managed to manoeuvre it towards a big isolated rock that towered from the sea-bed to a height just short of the surface. I then took as deep a breath as I could, and swam round the rock under water, hoping to meet the fish coming round the other way. It saw through my little trick, however, and when I saw it again it was advancing into the green and mysterious depths in quite a different direction.

When I turned the sharp edge of the rock I found myself confronted by creatures of quite a different kind. At the entrance to an irregularly shaped cavern immediately beneath me there were two big *budo* (the fish that we call 'crows'); I could see the big, strong, shiny, black backs of the creatures, which remained there motionless, uncertain what to do. Underneath the *budo*, on the sea-bed fifteen or twenty feet deeper, was a small octopus. Its swollen fleshy body was continually changing colour, as if expressing waves of different kinds of emotion; one moment it was greenish, the next it was yellow, now it was nearly red, then purple, and then yellow again. It gazed at me fixedly, and the emotion in its eyes was an almost tangible hatred. Meanwhile, it stretched out its long thin tentacles along the lumpy rock like a thief stretching out his hands for a jewel; then it retreated until it was almost hidden by the seaweed. The moment I spent looking at it was sufficient to allow the *budo* to vanish from view. For several seconds I could feel the vibration in the water caused by the flick of their departing tails.

I crossed a stretch of deep water and then found myself up against the almost vertical rock. The tumult of silvery water over my head was indescribably beautiful. Every wave caused a metallic crash, and a shower of little bubbles exploded downwards. But the noise above barely reached me; it was a silent tumult; pure form, a bedlam of light. When I emerged from a cloud of bubbles which prevented me for a moment from seeing where I was, in the distance, beyond some crevices in the rock, I saw a tail, which I recognized immediately; it was that of my dentex. I was tired now after the time I had spent fighting the waves and because of the water that entered the breathing tube, but I took a deep breath and went under again. Here the bottom was perhaps twelve or fifteen feet deep and very irregular. If I managed to get to the other side of two rocks yonder I should be able to surprise my prey. It seemed as if I should never get there, but I kept on, and did. The dentex did not see me. I fired my harpoon, and then went up for air without even waiting to see whether I had hit my mark. But I could tell at once that I had done so; the gun dragged in my hand.

I made my way wearily ashore, and expected Penny to exclaim with delight when she saw my prey, but I was disappointed.

'You cruel man!' she exclaimed. 'How would you like to be harpooned like that?'

I was too tired and cold to engage in an argument, particularly as I did not feel I was on very strong ground. Meanwhile the sun had come out again, and we walked slowly towards the Cape of Ebisu to rest for a while on the rocks.

By now it was late afternoon, and a number of boats were returning from the day's work. The sea was still choppy. The naked Ama girls manoeuvred the little boats skilfully between the rocks, using the single oar at the stern both to steer and to propel themselves with. Some of them waved to us cheerfully.

I had an idea.

'Penny, I said, 'I want you to do something. I want you to be a sacrifice for the cause.'

'Sacrifice? Do you mean you want to eat me? I'm too bony.'

'I want something much less dramatic of you.'

'What?'

'When we go back to the village I shall walk in front, and I want you to walk a few paces behind me, naked except for your slip.'

'I beg your pardon?'

'Don't you see the idea? If the Ama girls see a foreign woman behaving just as they do, they may end up by being less unapproachable.'

'Oh I see. Public relations by strip-tease. Is that the idea?'

'It may work. Shall we try it?'

The little procession entered the village soon afterwards. I walked in front with the big dentex on my back and my harpoon gun in my hand, and behind me a foreign woman wearing only her slip and looking as cool and self-possessed as if she were in a nudist camp.

It was the busiest moment of the day; everyone was hard at work about the boats drawn up on the shore or round the fresh-water wells. Before we had gone a hundred yards we were practically mobbed. Was it the naked woman that caused the excitement? Not on your life. Nobody took the slightest notice of poor Penny; at Hekura a naked woman is just about as surprising as a tree in a forest. But a fine dentex caught with that strange device, a harpoon gun, was a real sensation. The invisible wall that the Ama had so conscientiously built up round us collapsed like a house of cards, and they bombarded us, practically overwhelmed us, with questions. 'How did you catch that *tai*? How does that thing work? Will you sell it to us? How much is it? Show us how it works! . . .'

# Freedom of the City

So at last the spell was broken. Because of my harpoon gun the Ama dropped their reserve and suddenly showed a lively awareness of our existence. The last thing that I had expected was that it would happen like this. But persistence generally brings its own reward.

Next day the weather was bad, and a strong delegation of fishermen came to the temple to examine, discuss, and discover the secrets of the fabulous object.* As is usual on such occasions, the talk went on for hours. Innumerable tiny cups of tea were drunk, and the harpoon gun was taken to pieces and put together again and passed from hand to hand.

In the afternoon the weather improved a little, and it was arranged that an expedition of about twenty men and boys should put to sea for a demonstration. We crossed the island to one of the many beaches near the cape at the south-west corner, where large numbers of Ama women and girls were at work near the shore. Instead of disappearing, as they had always done in the past, when they saw us with their menfolk they gathered round to find out what we were up to. Who would have thought that my rusty old harpoon gun would have worked this magic? We got into a boat and went a little way out to sea.

'There are always *tai* where the Ama women work; they eat scraps of food dropped from the boats,' Shirosaki's eldest son, who was with us, announced.

No sooner were we in the water than we came across a lot of *tai* feeding. Many of the boys who came with us had brought primitive bamboo harpoons of the kind used in Polynesia, but I stopped them from using them in order not to frighten the fish. I was lucky. The first time I dived I harpooned a *tai*

* Plates 17, 18.

weighing nearly five pounds, and it was pulled into the boat to the accompaniment of guttural exclamations. Our triumph could not have been more complete. At the very least we were now honorary natives of the island.

What a difference there was now when we walked down the stony village path between the houses and the sea. Everyone greeted or smiled at us, and boys came running up to touch the miraculous contraption; and the Ama girls accepted us as if we belonged to their own people. Apart from the practical advantages and the fact that the prospect of making our film had suddenly grown much closer, it was delightful to feel, so to speak, adopted into the community of these sons and daughters of the sea.

In order to strike while the iron was hot, a strong deputation was formed, and went to the Shirosaki's house. It included Murata, and a friend, the painter Makino, who had meanwhile arrived from Tokyo, but not Penny.

The venerable uncrowned king of the island was squatting by his *irori* (the square hearth in the middle of the room), smoking a very long pipe with a minute bowl scarcely big enough to put one's finger in. The *irori* was full of pearly grey ash which had been scrupulously raked into straight lines, and in the middle of it was a handful of burning cinders which Shirosaki used to keep his pipe alight; this was a kind of domestic ritual carried out with slow and measured movements, expressing calm and confidence and total indifference to what might be happening in the outside world. Every now and then in the shadow at the sides of the room we caught a glimpse of the women of the household; Shirosaki's daughter-in-law, a charming, smiling and handsome woman of forty, or one or other of his granddaughters, Vàlkyries of the sea with mahogany-coloured skins.

Shirosaki received us with formal politeness, and became only slightly less unbending when he saw that we had brought him gifts. In Japan gifts are given on every visit, at every meeting, at every stage of all negotiations; and they have to be properly wrapped up in accordance with very definite rules.

Thus Shirosaki could not tell what the gifts were but, from the tone of our voices, the weight and size of the parcels, and the luxuriousness of the wrappings, he could not fail to conclude that we meant serious business. Moreover, he was not a man to waste time on the preliminary prolixities and preambles usual in this part of the world. A glance at his face, a basic landscape of dry, sawdust-coloured muscle, from which there protruded two sharp eyes, was sufficient to let one see he was a man who liked going straight to the point.

'I told you before that the girls earn a great deal at this time of year. I am prepared to put at your disposal a boat complete with six girls for the whole day in return for a suitable recompense.'

At this point Murata took up the thread, and a subtle verbal duel followed. Agreement having been reached in principle, all that remained was the question of the appropriate fee. On one side was Shirosaki, with few ideas in his head, each of them, however, as massive as a block of granite, which had to be destroyed or accepted as they stood; on the other Murata, advancing like a serpent, yielding and withdrawing again, and doing all in his power to catch his opponent out.

# Down to Work

IT was barely dawn when I got up and went out to look at the sea. I was terrified that the weather might turn out bad. Last night's sunset had been too Baroque for me to have been able to sleep peacefully. After the successful conclusion of yesterday's negotiations, with Ama girls at our disposal for filming, it simply must be fine. Fortunately it looked quite promising. The dark mass of Sado Island was visible more than fifty miles to the east, and this, according to the elders of Hekura, was a sure sign of good weather.

At about half past seven we went down to the harbour and found our boat and the Ama girls ready.

'Do you want the best or the prettiest?' Shirosaki had asked us the day before.

'Why? Can't the two things be combined?'

'No, it's most unusual. The prettiest are the young ones, and they are hardly ever very skilful. The best are over thirty.'

'So it's a myth that diving girls pass their prime early and die young?'

'It's a complete myth. Haven't you noticed how many old women there are? They start work at sixteen and keep at it every year until they are forty or forty-five, and they enjoy excellent health. Fatal accidents are very rare indeed. There was one two years ago when a girl's rope got caught on a rock under water. Everybody still talks about it.'

I asked Shirosaki the question that everybody asks when they hear about the Ama girls.

'But why do the women dive and not the men?'

'Because women are much tougher, of course. If we men stay in the water for two hours, we're half dead of cold, but women are not, they are covered with fat, like seals. Also they can hold their breath longer, and they're calmer. In the old days men used to dive too, but everybody knows that their work was less profitable, and so it would be today.'

These words of Shirosaki's were a reminder of the many long-distance swimming achievements (the Channel and the Great Lakes in America) which stand to the credit of women. A glance at our Ama girls was sufficient to show that Shirosaki was right. The selection was based on a compromise; we had two pretty girls and two skilful ones. The pretty ones were under twenty. They were gay and noisy, and seemed delighted at the opportunity of playing the film-star for a few hours. With their strong bodies, modelled by the sea, and their not very developed breasts, they recalled the Venus of Milo. The older, skilled women were obviously mothers, and they sat apart silently, as if wondering how long this farce was going to continue.

We set out in two boats loaded with fishing and filming equipment, baskets of food, and tubs for the *awabi*. A boy went in each boat. Assisting the diving girls is a male task. It is a responsible job, calling for constant attention and hard work; the most important part of it consists of holding the rope by which the diving girls are tied and pulling them up quickly when they tug to indicate that their breath is running out.

The sun gathered strength as it rose in the sky, and the day turned out to be magnificent; the blue of the calm sea was worthy of the Mediterranean. Conditions as perfect as this are rather rare in this part of the world; either the sky is clear and the wind blows up and makes the sea rough, or the sea is as flat as a pancake but the sky is overcast and rain threatens. I must point out here how privileged and spoilt are we southern Europeans, accustomed as we are to the calm water and blue skies of the Mediterranean; few seas in the world are as marvellous as the Tyrrhenian, the Ionian and, of course, the Aegean.

Because of the fine weather all Hekura turned out for a big day's work,* so it was an ideal opportunity of seeing the Ama

* Plate 38.

at work. A number of boats had already gone out and taken up position half a mile or even a mile from the shore. Others were still making ready. Often a motor-boat towed three, four or even five rowing-boats behind it.

After pushing off from the stony beach, we made for a point about a mile offshore to the south of the island, where a large number of boats had gathered. In this part of Japan boats are propelled by a single scull resting in a nick in the stern; the sculler stands, and uses a complicated, twisting stroke resembling that of the Venetian gondoliers; and the scull of course also serves as rudder. In our boat the work was done by one of the older Ama girls, a smiling, charming creature;* the other was propelled by a sturdy boy wearing a straw hat.

When we reached the other Ama boats we cast anchor and prepared for diving. Much of the sea-bed around Hekura consists of flats that slope gently downwards towards the ocean depths. Inshore the water is from nine to twelve feet deep; father out it descends to thirty, thirty-five, sixty feet and more. This submarine landscape, seen through one's mask, looks like a plain fading into the blue distance, with rocks, stones and pebbles scattered about. Here and there are bright patches of sand, and *Posidonia* seaweed grows abundantly. The *awabi* attach themselves to the rocks and isolated stones and are to be found where the seaweed is thickest. It is useless to try to detect them from the surface; you have to go to the bottom and grope for them with your hands among the stones and submarine vegetation.

I asked one of the girls how the diving sites were apportioned. She said that the rule was first come, first served, and that there were hardly ever any disputes. However, *awabi* were getting scarcer every year; perhaps too many divers were after them. They were having to go deeper and deeper every year and there were some who went down to sixty feet. At that depth the work was very tiring, and you could stay at the bottom only for a few moments.

* Plate 43.

Before entering the water the girls put on goggles equipped with small, pear-shaped rubber bulbs, by squeezing which the air pressure between the glass and the girl's eyes can be equalized. Before entering the water the girls also tie round their waists a rope about sixty feet long by which they are hauled to the surface at the end of their dive; when the girl gives a tug, her assistant in the boat pulls her up as fast as he can. Finally they tie round their waists a belt loaded with lumps of lead to serve as ballast and, like a warrior putting on his sword, they stick in their belt a sharp iron tool (*tegane*) which serves to detach the *awabi* shells from the rock (Plates 44–49, 63–71).

Very soon we were all in the water; the girls started looking for *awabi*, and I started looking for film-shots. The sea-bed beneath us was typical of Hekura; a plain scattered about with pearly grey rocks and clumps and fields of *Posidonia*. The water was very clear and rather cold and about thirty feet deep. After swimming a few strokes beneath the surface I looked up: the keel of the boat resembled a cut in a silvery ceiling that was in continual motion like a living thing. Next to the boat two Ama girls lay on the surface like strange insects, looking down at the sea-bed. Then one of them made up her mind. Her head vanished for a moment above the silver ceiling (no doubt to take a deep breath) and then immediately reappeared; her body arched, and with a movement of her hips she began her rapid dive.*

When she reached bottom she started groping among the seaweed.† The greeny blue or brownish *Posidonia* is familiar to everybody; it is the commonest seaweed on our coasts also. Here it was thick and abundant enough frequently almost to conceal the diver's body, leaving only her back visible. Then she took her metal tool in her right hand and placed it against the rock on the underside of a projection; this action caused her to turn right over, and for a moment she was face upwards. But now her breath was running short. She tugged,

* Plate 53.

† Plate 57.

and was quickly pulled up. In her hands she had two fine *awabi*, and she held her legs together and her arms to her sides to offer a minimum of resistance. A silvery triangle of air bubbles came from her nostrils.*

When they reach the surface the Ama girls hold on to the side of the boat to rest for a moment and give a characteristic whistle (*ama-bui*). A dive lasts for forty-five or fifty seconds, or sometimes for a whole minute. After about twenty dives, or an hour's work, the girls climb into the boat and rest for half an hour or so. If the sky is overcast, or if it is cold, a wood fire is lit in the brazier in the middle of the boat and the girls cover themselves with a crude embroidered kimono, forming a kind of cloak. At midday they either stay in the boat or go ashore for their lunch and take a longer rest in the sun. Then they go back to work until four or five o'clock. Such is the Ama girls' working day.

Obviously it is very hard work. Diving now and again for the pleasure of underwater fishing is one thing; doing it day after day from June to September, often when the weather is bad or cold, is quite another. However, never in my life have I seen healthier-looking people than the Ama. Their bodies bronzed by sun and wind are the image of primordial humanity, remote indeed from the soft, whitish creatures who live under smoky skies in cities. Ama women live to a great age, apparently unaffected by the nature of their work and the apnoea to which they are subjected during the course of many years.

Near our boat were others with other crews of Ama girls. From my underwater vantage-point I could see them in every direction, descending to the bottom or mounting to the surface like shadows in the blue submarine haze. One of the most fascinating features of the submarine world is its silence; it is not for nothing that J.-Y. Cousteau called his great book *The Silent World*. There was something enchanted and fairy-like about the spectacle of these human beings flitting to and fro between the sea-bed and the silvery surface; the

* Plate 56.

only sound was that of metal *tegane* being tapped against the rocks to detach the *awabi*.

Unfortunately I was without breathing apparatus, and what would have been a lot of very fine shots were impossible wearing an ordinary mask and simply holding one's breath. A long submarine travelling among the Ama girls at work would undoubtedly have been magnificent. That day at least two hundred must have been diving in our immediate area alone.

The girls were often very beautiful. Their strong, graceful bodies glided through the water with the naturalness of creatures moving about in their own element. Particularly impressive was the skill of the older women, who were generally much less attractive, showing the traces of numerous child-births. The young were often very dashing, and sometimes wasted precious energy larking about with each other, and every now and again they would make jerky, ungraceful movements; but the older women, with years of experience behind them which had become second nature, moved about in the water with a minimum of physical effort, saving their breath with great skill; above all they used their eyes and their intelligence, floating lightly between rocks and seaweed and infallibly making for the favourite hiding-places of the *awabi*.

The crew of one boat near ours consisted of a mother aged little more than thirty and a daughter of sixteen; the responsibility of handling the rope was in the hands of a young son or brother aged thirteen or fourteen.

## Filming Under Difficulties

We went on filming, with interruptions, for about a fortnight. With the surface shots we had no trouble, but with the underwater shots we kept running into difficulties. In the first place we were hampered by our makeshift, primitive equipment. I had no breathing apparatus, and the shooting had to be restricted to the short periods during which I could hold my breath; and I had to do everything single-handed, because Murata and Takahashi were able to help only in the boat.

The apparatus consisted of a camera in a metal container with a transparent window in front of the lens. To make it as simple as possible, no device for reloading under water had been included, with the result that it had to be taken on board and opened at the end of every reel. Filming in such conditions was obviously a long and wearisome business.

On top of this every single shot required a whole concatenation of favourable circumstances, many of which tended to be exceedingly capricious. First of all, the Ama girls had to be available, and this involved daily negotiations with old Shirosaki, who was always demanding additional fees and presents; these negotiations were sometimes very difficult indeed. Then, if sequences taken on different days were to have any meaning, it was obviously necessary to have the same girls every day. But what tended to happen in practice was that if one day our stars had been, say, Yoshiko and Noriko, next day Hanako and Yuriko would turn up with a smile, explaining that the other girls had had to go to Wajima for a permanent wave, or that their mothers were ill.

Even when all these obstacles had been surmounted, there were at least three other conditions which had to be right before we could do any shooting. The sea had to be calm, the water had to be clear, and the sun had to shine. The coincidence of these three things turned out to be pretty rare. If the sea were calm the sky would be overcast, if the water was clear there would be waves, and then, just when everything seemed to be perfect, a bank of clouds would blow up, spoil the light, and darken the sea-bed.

However, working with the Ama was a pleasure. I have never known girls more willing and co-operative. They cheerfully did whatever was asked of them, and did not mind staying in the water for hours if necessary. But they were not in the habit of thinking, and all their movements had to be tried out, corrected, and then tried out again before they could be shot. Meanwhile the sea, which had been calm and clear when we started work, would start getting rough or the visibility would deteriorate for some unknown reason; or, worse still, the sun would disappear for good behind a bank of cloud. It was a miracle if a whole day's work resulted in a few inches of usable film.

However, gradually we made progress, and soon we could claim to have completed the essential framework. How exciting it was to see the finished product for the first time in Rome a few months later. The running time was only a few minutes—the concentrated result of hours of exhausting labour. On the whole it was satisfactory, and some fleeting aspects of a highly specialized, venturesome, and strikingly beautiful human condition had been captured.

## Nakano-san

At the end of August there were two or three days of very high seas. A furious gale from the north, from Siberia, causing mountainous waves to crash against the rocks, the offshore islets, and the rocky shore that faced the open sea. It was like living on a ship; there was nowhere in the island where you could get away from the howl and roar. The deep, distant boom of the breakers was almost frighteningly audible even in Demura, the part of the village facing the sheltered little harbour. The wind whistled in the wires, or came in gusts and eddies, raising clouds of dust and sand, enough to blind anyone bold enough to venture along the path of grey stones.

Few islanders were to be seen abroad while the gale lasted. Occasionally a woman with her head muffled in a big handkerchief was to be seen using a primitive device to press seaweed which had been dried in the sun; and you caught glimpses of the men in their houses mending their nets and tackle.

The temple, exposed to the full force of the gale on its little eminence, creaked and groaned. The windows rattled, the roof creaked, the walls seemed about to collapse. The small oases of calm that were to be found behind a house or in the shelter of a wall or under a hollow rock were exceedingly inviting, particularly if the sun came out for a few minutes, as happened every now and then. Low clouds chased each other across the pale grey sky.

In one of these oases in the shelter of a big, grey, porous volcanic rock we came across Nakano-san repairing a small boat. Nakano-san, as I mentioned earlier, was over seventy, but he looked ten or fifteen years younger. It was impossible to imagine a better, simpler, or more honest man than Nakano-san; he was the best type of straightforward, old-style Japanese. We had used him as boatman and general handy-man ever since our arrival in Hekura. Today he seemed particularly depressed.

'What is the matter, Nakano-san?' we asked. 'This gale won't last for ever, it's not the end of the world by a long way, and your grandsons will soon be able to go back to work.'

'The gale?' he answered. 'It would make no difference if the sea were calm. There are some things that are not so easily remedied.'

'What is it, then?'

Nakano-san went on fashioning a new floorboard for the boat with a kind of knife.

'You see this boat, *danna-san*? It was my son's. I swore never to use it again; I wanted to keep it only in memory of him. But we are poor people, and now we have to use it all the same. I can't work on it without thinking about Takeshi. What is the good of an old man without a son? *Muda-na seikatsu da*, what is the good of living?'

We tried to find some words of comfort for Nakano-san. But it was like trying to fill an abyss with handfuls of sand. Nakano-san's son, we were told, would now have been thirty; he was killed during the war in the Philippines while still in his teens. The old fisherman and his son had always been tremendously devoted to each other, and after all these years the wound was still bleeding.

## Evening with the Hosomichi

THE time passed quickly. Shooting a film in these conditions was arduous and exhausting, and at the end of the day all we were capable of was eating our evening meal and flinging ourselves on our beds to sleep.

The nature by which we were surrounded kept us constant company. There was the sea in all its humours and in every conceivable variation of light, both above and below the surface; there were the wind and the vast horizons; the ever-changing clouds; the starry nights and the tranquil dawns; and the sunsets. One morning we saw a most extraordinary cloud formation; the sky was lined with huge streaks of mother-of-pearl cirrus at an immense height and looking slightly unreal; one by one these great streaks were distorted by a transverse wind into strange and striking scimitars.

Gradually we made friends with many of the islanders.

We spent a number of evenings with the Buddhist priest and his wife.* The conversation was not very brilliant. Both Mr. and Mrs. Takada were people of few words, and the evenings used to end with our all reading or doing our own work. But their company was by no means disagreeable. While we worked on our accounts, or planned the next day's shooting, Mrs. Takada corrected her pupils' exercise books by the light of a petrol lamp while her husband worked on the history of Hekura he was compiling; or sometimes he would be busy on a *kyokatabira*, which is the name given to the special kimono in which the dead are buried. This is worn in the manner opposite to the normal; that is to say, left over right in the case of men and right over left in the case of women. The priest's work consisted of writing Buddhist prayers with a thin brush on the white material. *Namu Kwannon Bosatsu*,

* Plates 24, 25.

*Namu Amida Bosatsu, Namu Seishi Bosatsu,** he wrote. He would spend hours over this task, as if he were a miniaturist.

The burial customs of the Ama are interesting, but differ only in detail from those of the mainland. The body is always laid out with the head towards the north, clothed in a *kyokatabira* and with a head-covering bearing religious inscriptions. A small bag (*maidare*) is laid on the breast containing a coin to pay for the passage over the *Sai-no-Kawara*, the Buddhist Lethe.

The members of the Hosomichi household were exactly the opposite of this serious, studious, and slightly gloomy young couple.

On our way home one afternoon Penny cut her foot on a splinter. An old woman promptly appeared at the threshold of her house with a basin of water, and when the cut had been washed she invited us inside. We were at the end of the village, near the Taka-dokoro, where the poorest inhabitants lived, and the kitchen was very different from that of the Shirosaki household. It was a smoky cavern of old timber, which was as black as pitch and in places had been worn until it was shiny by heaven knows how many generations of Ama. Round the *irori* were sitting four or five old men of a kind that no longer exist anywhere in the world. They were nearly naked and very dark-skinned as the result of a lifetime of exposure to sun and sea water; and they all had white, shaggy beards of various lengths. They were smoking and telling each other funny stories; every now and then they burst into uproarious laughter. They received us with the delightful naturalness and dignity of true primitives.

The most aged of these aged men, all lines and wrinkles, was Hosomichi. He offered us tea, and then invited us to take a bath.

'It's ready now, you go first.'

* 'Let us worship the Bodhisattva (Bosatsu) Kwannon, the Bodhisattva Amida, and the Bodhisattva Seishi'; *i.e.* (in Sanskrit) Avalokitesvara, Amitabha, and Mahasthamaprapta. Seishi and Kwannon attend on Amida and, according to popular belief, with him visit the death-beds of the pious and welcome them to paradise. (See Sir Charles Eliot, *Japanese Buddhism*, London, 1935, p. 355.)

'No, let the lady go first.'

'What? Do you let women go first in your part of the world?'

'That is our custom.'

'Did you hear that? Did you hear that?' the old man exclaimed. 'But that is the end, that really is the end!'

There followed a cavernous peal of laughter dating from about 20,000 B.C.

'I don't see that there's anything to laugh at,' I remarked. 'You Ama depend entirely on your womenfolk, don't you? Where would you be without your women *awabi* gatherers?'

'That's true enough. But let them bath first? That would be shameful! Where are we?'

Penny was somewhat alarmed at the shouting and laughter and gnome-like movements of this aged chorus. She had no desire to be the first to try the bath, and insisted on my doing so.

It consisted of a huge vessel of the kind in which fishing-nets are dyed to make them more resistant to brine, and was housed in a den full of ropes, oars, anchors, and tackle. A wood fire that filled the place with smoke was burning underneath it. At the bottom of the vessel a circular piece of wood had been placed to prevent your feet and buttocks from coming into contact with the hot metal. What a bath! However, after a day in the sea the fresh water was marvellously relaxing and refreshing.

We went back to the temple for dinner, but later, after acquiring a bottle of *saké* in the village, we went back to call on the Hosomichi again. The old men were still gathered round the hearth by the light of the petrol lamp, and the women of the house were there too; two or three crones and some girls, obviously *awabi* divers.

It was an extremely gay and noisy evening, at any rate for us men. The women, squatting in the darkest corners of the room, chatted among themselves, and the young ones often put their hands to their mouths to stifle their laughter. Penny, who liked falling in with local usage, sat with the women, conducting a halting conversation on methods of cooking seaweed.

# Welcoming the Dead

In Japan three days are set aside annually for the remembrance of the dead. There is a similar day of remembrance in the Christian world, but there could not be a greater contrast between the spirit of the two. With us the dead are remembered in cold, damp, gloomy November, as if to emphasize the sadness of the occasion; in Japan *o-bon* is celebrated at the height of summer, when the sun reappears after the rainy season and the colours are at their brightest and most magnificent. At this season the planting out of the rice has been completed, there is a kind of pause in the Japanese agricultural year, and the Japanese remember those who have preceded them into the mystery of death.

But the differences go deeper than the weather. The fundamental attitude to death in the two cases is so totally different as to be almost opposite. From the most ancient times the Japanese have had the charming belief that for the three days of *o-bon* the dead return to the land of the living and resume their lifetime occupations; they must therefore be received cheerfully and happily, like welcome guests. So the house is thoroughly spring-cleaned in their honour, tables are laid with food and drink for their refreshment, and their lifetime tastes and interests are scrupulously recalled. If, for instance, grandpa was fond of painting, paper and a brush are laid out for him near the *tokonoma* (the corner reserved for works of art); or if that young nephew who died of a sudden illness during his student days was a passionate mountain-climber, his ice-axe is laid out for him. Above all, the dead must not be received with glum faces. Any tears that are shed must be shed in secret. These are not days of mourning, but a gay festival.

Throughout the three days of *o-bon* Japan is full of dance

62. *It is a pleasure to go back into the water in the warm afternoon sunshine.*

63, 64. *Getting ready for the plunge.*

64

65

66

65, 66, 67, 68. *Taeko, of Mikuria, one of the Seven Islands, gets ready for work in the deep water that surrounds the black rock on which she lives during the summer months.*

67

68

71. *Lead ballast helps the diver in her descent to the depths.*

and song. It is also a favourite occasion for processions and for theatrical performances, particularly in the country. Japanese popular traditions are displayed in all the inexhaustible wealth of their regional and local variations, and they are always very colourful.

In towns *o-bon* is generally celebrated in mid-July, but in the country, which for many purposes still remains faithful to the lunar calendar, it takes place towards the middle of August. In the general confusion of customs that is so typical of our times advantage is sometimes taken of the variations in date to celebrate the same occasion twice. In Hekura *o-bon* is celebrated at the end of August, when the *awabi* fishing season is nearly over. The most important Shinto ceremony of the year, the procession to the shrine dedicated to the Princess of the Hidden Bay, takes place at the same season.

The Japanese are always early risers, and on festival days they rise even earlier than usual, and activities begin long before dawn. On August 26th the Buddhist priest woke us at 4 a.m.; the temple had to be ready before first light, when the congregation would be arriving for the *o-mairi* ('honourable visit'), one of the ceremonies connected with the dead. The congregation, as in Italy, was largely feminine. Before six o'clock the temple was crowded with Ama women of all ages.

In Japan Buddhist ceremonies seem nearly always to attract more women than men, while Shinto ceremonies seem to attract more men than women, whether young or old. I am speaking, of course, of popular religion, as expressed in ordinary family usage, not of responses to definite spiritual needs.

It is difficult to suggest a simple explanation of this religious difference between the sexes. The spirituality of Buddhism may make a more immediate appeal to women; the spectacular rites of Shinto, often involving feats of strength and endurance (such as the protracted drumming by Toshio Mifune in the film *The Rickshaw Man*) appeal to a specifically masculine spirit. It should not be forgotten that many Shinto festivals have the same significance to the Japanese as have meetings of the fire brigade or the municipal band in the villages of the South Tirol, at any rate in so far as they subtly express the individual's integration in the community.

The ceremony lasted for a long time. The priest, dressed in magnificent gilded robes, chanted in a sonorous voice that you would never have attributed to him if you had heard only his speaking voice, and read from the sacred writings (a *sutra*). This was followed by an anthem to which the congregation gave the responses.

Next day the whole island was decorated in honour of the occasion. Though the weather was excellent and the sea as flat as a pancake, nobody went out to work. The men sat at the entrance to their houses, doing odd jobs connected with their boats, and the women washed themselves at the wells, and poured buckets of water over each other with cheerful bursts of laughter, while others, already in their best clothes, found excuses to pay calls and show off and admire each other's new *yukata* (light summer kimono). The children were carefully washed and combed, and a lot of them were actually dressed. A number of boats were decorated with bright colours. The annual procession round the island was due in the afternoon.

At about eleven o'clock we went to the Shinto shrine, or *miya*. The ideogram for *miya* also means 'palace', but there was nothing palatial about this building, at any rate to western eyes. The exterior was nothing but a great solid dry stone wall, looking rather like an embankment. From a distance, from the sea, for instance, it suggested a primitive, prehistoric fortress. In a quiet, sunny courtyard inside, sheltered from the gales, were two timber structures to which time and weather had given a pleasing mother-of-pearl patina. The bigger of the two sheltered the *mikoshi*, the elaborate gilded palanquin used for carrying about the *shintai*, or 'body' of the god; the *shintai* was a metal mirror. The inconspicuous smaller structure constituted the 'holy of holies'.

The structure in which the *mikoshi* was kept was obviously

treated as a kind of local museum, a sanctum devoted to the island's past glories. It contained prints of sailing and other ships, an ancient oleograph of a British sailing ship, portraits of the Emperor and Empress of Japan, scenes from the Russo–Japanese War, the works of the thirty-six poets, etc. Two huge *awabi* were displayed on a table, as well as a number of strange shells, two mythological wooden carvings, a metal mirror, and a large number of *gohei*, *i.e.* paper ornaments which take the place of the offerings of silk and linen made in sacred places in ancient times.

The *mikoshi*, the big palanquin, was exceptionally fine. I was told that it was two hundred years old. However, last year a prosperous Ama had had it completely refurbished at great expense; it had been regilded and relacquered (Plate 7). I was also told that it weighed at least six hundredweight.

The ceremonies began in the early afternoon. The *mikoshi* was brought out and laid on two trestles. It was to be carried round the island by fifteen of the strongest young islanders; these youths were dressed as women, and a lot of them actually wore make-up. This wearing of women's clothes is certainly a feature of great anthropological interest, but I have not succeeded in discovering a satisfactory explanation for it. Two relevant facts may be that the ceremonies were being held in honour of a goddess, and that we were among the Ama, with whom women occupy a much more important position than they do in the rest of Japanese society. Beside the *mikoshi* there gathered all the notables of Hekura, fishermen and owners of fishing vessels, grave men looking like gnarled old tree-trunks, with the serious expression on their lined faces that is characteristic of simple people on solemn occasions. Also present were two *kannushi* (Shinto priests). One was the priest normally resident in the island; the other had come specially from Wajima. The archaic cut of their simple robes suggested the Japan of fifteen centuries ago.

The *kannushi* of Hekura was a kindly, smiling man, half fisherman himself, rather like a parish priest who shares with his flock the trials and tribulations and simple pleasures of the daily struggle with nature.* His counterpart from Wajima was a younger, much more elegant personage, obviously a specialist in liturgical matters; his long, slender, delicate hands immediately struck one as being those of a fastidious ritualist. It would have been hard for an individual of this type not to look down on the crude people by whom he was now surrounded and this poor colleague of his stranded here on this island rock in the middle of the sea beyond the confines of the civilized world; and by every gesture and every look he betrayed his secret thoughts in the matter.

As soon as everyone had assembled and squatted on little mats laid on the stones, the *kannushi* of Wajima produced a flute from a silk handkerchief and started playing it, to a drum accompaniment. Some moments of unforgettable enchantment followed. The thin, rather melancholy music, in which poignant lamentation was mingled with moments of sudden joy, like glimpses of the sun in a dark forest, faded into the immensity of the silence. The only sound that came from beyond the great stone walls was the faint roar of the waves beating on the shore.

When the music was over, the *kannushi* from Wajima carefully wrapped up his flute in the silk handkerchief and read a long sacred text in a finely modulated voice which sounded highly sophisticated in these primitive surroundings. Then he rose to his feet in a rather self-satisfied manner and waved in the air an *onosa*, a stick with paper decorations to ward off devils and evil spirits. Finally he caused *saké* (rice wine) to be distributed to everybody present.

There was a short pause, and then the procession was formed. In front went the notables, bearing fans, pennants and flags. Then came the *mikoshi*, six hundredweight of gilded and lacquered wood with gilded ornamentation, silk curtains, and a silk phoenix on top, the whole carried on the shoulders of fifteen singing young men. Fourteen lanterns came next, one for each *kuni* (district) of the island, and then the rest of the islanders, young and old, venerable seniors and little boys,

* Plate 29.

women of every age, robust young diving girls, bent old women, many with their grandchildren, and little girls dressed in bright colours.

The procession passed under the big *torii* (Plate 21) and made its way across the nearly deserted beach of Owada towards the village—a river of colour and ample robes flying in the wind. The sun had come out again, and bright little clouds were sailing in the sky; the afternoon, which a short time previously had seemed old and tired, grey and fusty, had undergone a sudden rejuvenation. The voices of the young men, the shouting of the children, the music of a flute, were lost in all the immensity, carried away by the breath of the sea. There was no distracting element in the picture, nothing extraneous to remind one of other human activities or circumstances or purposes; this was just a procession along the seashore in the purest and most absolute sense.

Soon the houses became more numerous, closer together, and bigger and richer; we were entering the village. The crowd grew gay and noisy. Every hundred yards or so the young men laid the heavy palanquin on two trestles and rested, and people from the neighbouring houses hurried to offer them *saké*, of which they drank little cupful after little cupful. After half a mile they were in a state of blissful merriment. The palanquin advanced now slowly, now quickly, lunging and swerving to right or left, or turning completely in its tracks, or sometimes spinning like a top.

'It goes where the gods want it to,' an old man explained to me.

Gradually the afternoon turned into evening. The sun went on shining, and it grew warmer and sultrier. The sea reflected the sun's rays like a glittering cauldron, and the palanquin continued its crazy way, pursuing an ever more erratic course, to the huge delight of the children and scattering young Ama girls to right and left, bringing the divine blessing to houses and people, boats and tackle.

By sunset the procession had reached the other end of the island, the isthmus leading to the rock on which the shrine of Ebisu stands. The sun sank below the horizon like a huge red, almost animal-like, disk between layers of grey cloud. The wind had freshened and was disturbing the surface of the sea, which was darkening in colour. You breathed in lungfuls of brine, and voices were smothered by the sound of waves breaking on the rocks. From a distance the palanquin could be seen advancing against the light like a great beast with innumerable human legs as in a dance. The rest of the crowd remained behind and waited.

At the Ebisu shrine some simple rites were performed, and then the procession reformed for the return journey. By now it was nearly dark. *Chochins* (lanterns) were lit and stood out against the clear sky, in which the first stars appeared. All the house doors were open, red tongues of flame were visible in the kitchens, and lanterns shone over the doors. There was just enough light to enable one more or less to find one's way about, but the night swallowed up men, women and children, the palanquin, the notables and the *kannushi*, giving everything the vagueness of a dream. Gusts of wind brought one loud snatches of song, which as suddenly faded again. The thing had ceased to be a procession, and had become a strange and magical event on the borders of space and time. Only the sea seemed vast and immutable as ever.

Finally the Yashiro was reached and the *mikoshi* was put in the water, and there took place the blessing of the sea and all that lived in and by it. This was the culminating point of the festival, the culmination of the Ama religious year. The crowd seemed very excited, and was in a state of continual motion. Groups of boys and girls, men and women, families and their neighbours, continually formed and reformed. The young men carrying the palanquin were now completely drunk, and every step they took endangered the life and limbs of those in its immediate neighbourhood. To the accompaniment of loud shouts and cries, singing and complaints it was somehow or other manoeuvred down to the water. And then, to the accompaniment of undiminished din and confusion, it was carried back to the space in front of the Yashiro, where it was to remain for the night.

All that now remained was to go home slowly, singing.

An hour later there was another assembly, this time for men only; it was an extremely merry affair, with music in the form of a continuous and violent beating of a drum. Heaven knows how long the dancing and shouting, the games and singing, would have lasted if the weather had not suddenly changed again. The wind rose, and heavy rain started to fall. The paper lanterns got wet and disintegrated, and the little candles inside them went out.

Outside the sea continued to roar.

# Honourable Little Boat

AUGUST 28TH was the last day of *o-bon*. After the stormy night the sea grew calm again. The dead had spent three days with the living, and the time had come to bid them farewell again. Mysteriously they had emerged from the sea, and equally mysteriously they were returning to it. The sea is the Ama's home, from which they emerge and to which they return again.

I went to see Nakano-san, who lived only a few yards from the temple. The old man was busy making a little boat of grass and cane (Plates 9, 10).

'What are you doing, Nakano-san?'

'Today is the last day of *o-bon*. My dead son will be returning to the sea, so I am making him a boat. As you see, you take all the offerings that stood for three days at the family shrine—rice, beans, fruit, sweets and flowers—and wrap them in a *suzuki** mat, which you then work into the shape of a boat; then you add mast, rudder, yards, and coloured flags.'

Nakano-san, aided by his granddaughters, spent hours making his boat (*o-shoryo-bune*, 'honourable little boat of the shadows'). Not till after midday was he ready to go down to the water and consign it to the waves, pouring fresh water over it from a tin teapot. It was a moving moment. Nakano-san's granddaughters came with a rosary and muttered prayers, and the old man stood motionless on the stony shore. Goodbye, my son returning to the sea, goodbye till next year. Where are you going? What are you? What sort of ghostly life do you lead in the green depths? And who will there be to remember you if next year I am no longer here?

The festival came to an end during the afternoon. The big procession with the palanquin set out from the Yashiro, made

* *Suzuki* is a kind of esparto grass with strong leaves.

another tour of the village, again blessed the sea, and then the palanquin was taken back to the shrine from which it came.

After dark I discovered by chance that the two *kannushi*, accompanied by about twenty men and a lot of lanterns, were going to the Ebisu shrine. The sea had suddenly risen again, the wind came howling in from Siberia, and this made the going very difficult, particularly on the isthmus between the island and the rocks of the Taka-dokoro. However, we managed to reach the little shrine—a wooden hut with a little altar and two candles which flickered even when the door was shut.

Men only were present; tanned and weather-beaten fishermen wearing *yukata*. The *kannushi* from Wajima stood out among them like a hot-house plant. I was able to observe him closely for the first time. He no longer had the bored and superior air of the day before. He wore a purple silk robe, and on his head was a *kammuri*; he might have stepped straight from a page of Lady Murasaki or from a scroll with illustrations of ancient court ceremonial.

For several long minutes silence prevailed. The roar of the waves dashing on the rocks and the furious howling of the wind filled the little hut. Then, the *kannushi* from Wajima with elegant measured movements produced his flute from a black case and started to play. It was a thin trickle of music, sweet and sad, thoughtful and tender, ancient and almost feminine—like a ray of moonlight seen on emerging from a forest. The sturdy, tousle-haired, knotty-handed fishermen stood motionless, gazing into the void.

# Taeko

AFTER the festival we decided to make an excursion to the Seven Islands, so as not to leave this part of Japan with anything unexplored. The trip was well worth while. These austere, contorted rocks yielded nothing to Hekura either in natural beauty or in the quality of their Ama girls.

We set out before dawn in a stinking motor-boat and an angry sea. A slow swell was coming in from the ocean, the last relic of some distant storm. Our little boat interminably mounted the watery slopes and, pitching and tossing, slowly descended the other side. Meanwhile, threatening weather was blowing up from the east, and soon a furious wind arose, churning up steep little waves travelling in a completely different direction. The consequence was a chaotic, witch's cauldron of a sea, with waves at cross-purposes, now mounting to steep, foaming, threatening crests, now forming sudden, steep abysses into which we plunged as if we were going to be swallowed up.

We reached Mikuria, the biggest of the Seven Islands, wet through and green in the face. The sky was so black, and such a gale was blowing, that our boatman wanted to go back at once. He said that if the weather got worse we might be stranded for a week. However, I insisted on remaining. My obstinacy was rewarded, for soon afterwards the weather began to improve.

The ideograms for Mikuria mean 'honourable kitchen', but this probably represents a phonetic adaptation of a pre-existing name of unknown origin; Rome, for instance, is indicated in Japanese by two characters of which the first means 'bird-net' and the second 'horse', but no etymologist, whatever vagaries he might be capable of, would suggest that the word 'Rome' meant 'bird-net horse'.

Mikuria looks like a huge green rock rising abruptly out of the sea, but in reality its substance consists of black volcanic rock; but this is completely overgrown with luxuriant weeds and *sasá*, a kind of dwarf bamboo. It is a tiny island twisted into strange and surprising shapes, and the sea-bed all round is apocalyptic—full of submerged palaces sinking into the vivid dark blue of the deep water. There is one small beach, where there are some strange caves and a cluster of poor houses; and in the fine season thirty or forty Ama families live there (Plates 1, 3).

At Mikuria everything is more primitive, wilder, and poorer than at Hekura, but the Ama are more hospitable than those of the bigger island. It took only half an hour and a very modest gift to persuade Ito-san, the senior fisherman of Mikuria, to put at our disposal a boat with five Ama girls, all of them prettier and probably more skilful than those of Hekura. Their greater skill is easy to account for. At Mikuria the sea-bed is much more difficult and demanding than that at Hekura. Incidentally *fuka*, or shark, seem to be present in these parts, though I was assured by a venerable old woman that they never attacked the diving girls.

Towards midday the weather improved and—suddenly, as happens in these parts—the sea quietened down and in the lee of the island there were some areas of flat calm. We used the opportunity to take some more film, taking advantage in particular of our unforeseen encounter with the beautiful Taeko. In reality I suppose it was only right and proper that Mikuria, the most striking and dramatic of the islands, should conceal among its rock walls and black pinnacles, its green domes and mysterious caverns, the most superb of all the Ama girls.

Taeko was eighteen, and had been diving for two years. With her gaiety, innocence, and playfulness, she was truly delightful. She plummeted to such giddy, deep, dark depths as almost to disappear from the view of those remaining on the surface. Gentle, smiling, and slightly plump as she was, she presented a striking contrast to the harshness and severity of her surroundings. But that applied only to her appearance; her character—so far as we could judge from the short time we spent working with her—seemed to be in entire harmony with the jagged rocks and fierce, swirling waters of Mikuria. None of the other Ama girls dived as deep as the fearless and confident Taeko.

'What is it like down there, Taeko?' I asked.

'Wonderful, absolutely wonderful,' she replied. 'Sometimes it's a bit *sabishi* (lonely), particularly if there's a *fuka* swimming about.'

'Don't you get nervous?'

'*Fuka* never touch us Ama girls.'

Evening fell early over the Seven Islands. We went back to the little harbour and took Taeko and her companions home. Before leaving we climbed to the highest point of the island. It was nearly sunset. The sea shone like liquid fire. The six other islands of the little archipelago were all visible, some near, some farther away. There was Akashima ('Red Island'); Oshima ('Big Island'); Tatsu-jima ('Dragon Island'); as well as Eboshi-jima,* Aramiko-jima,† and Karimata-jima.‡ Strange and sonorous names for strange, impregnable rocks. Taeko was with us.

'They are my islands,' she said. 'Have you ever seen anything more beautiful anywhere?'

We were enchanted with Mikuria, at which we spent less than a day. Farewell, Ito-san, white-bearded patriarch in a torn shirt; farewell, Taeko of the green depths; farewell, Ama girls born of the sea! No other rock in all the world will remain such an enchanting memory.

* Isle shaped like an *eboshi* (ancient ceremonial head-dress).

† Isle of the god Ara.

‡ Isle shaped like a double-pointed arrow.

# Farewells, Formal and Otherwise

THE time had come to leave Hekura, the Seven Islands, and the Ama girls, and to return to the mainland—to so-called civilized life—offices, business suits, and ties.

The first signs of autumn were in the air. Hekura is on the same latitude as the Aegean Islands, but because of the neighbourhood of Siberia the climate is more like that of an island in the upper Adriatic. In winter, I was told, there is a great deal of snow and it is bitterly cold. It already felt uncomfortably cool in the shade without a sweater; and it was definitely a pleasure to feel the strong sun on one's skin. The Ama girls were going on diving for a few days yet, but the *awabi* season was as good as over.

We went to say goodbye to Shirosaki and his family. The exchanges of courtesy were rather formal, because the old man had never completely reconciled himself to the presence of strangers in his little realm. He had profited from our visit, for we had given him money and gifts, but the greed of ignorance certainly made him think that we could just as well have given him twice as much. The Buddhist priest and his wife were similarly formal; we had had no trouble with them, but the presence in their temple of strangers with a vast pile of equipment must certainly have been a nuisance to them at times.

Our parting from Nakano-san, however, was entirely different. He appeared alongside the fishing-boat that was to take us back to Wajima in his new boat. the boat that had belonged to his son, which he had sworn never to use, but to keep only in his memory; and he shook hands with us, which is very unusual for a Japanese, and actually wept. Goodbye Nakano-san, who knows if we shall ever meet again? He was a good, honest, simple man, and nobody better deserved happiness than he.

At the last moment, we heard an uproar from the end of the mole; it was caused by Hosomichi coming to say goodbye to us with his escort of wild old men. He brought us some huge *awabi* shells as a parting gift, and he wore one of them over his face, like a mask.

## Some Books about the Ama

SEGAWA KYOKO. *Ama-ki* ('The Book of the Ama Women'), Tokyo, 1942.

SEGAWA KYOKO AND SUZUKI JIRO. *Wajima Amamachi no Shakai Seikatsu no Hensen* ('Changes in Social Life in the Ama Village of Wajima'), in *Noto: Shizen, Bunka, Shakai* ('The Noto Peninsula. Aspects of Its Nature, Culture, and Social Life'), Tokyo, 1956, pp. 276–296.

YANAGIDA KUNIO. *Kaison Seikatsu no Kenkyu* ('Studies in the Life of Fishing Villages'), Tokyo, 1949.

YANAGIDA KUNIO. *Minzoku-gaku Jiten* ('Ethnological Dictionary'), Tokyo, 1954. (Note in particular article on the Ama.)

KANASAKI, H. *Hekura-jima to sono Ama no Seikatsu* ('The Island of Hekura and the Life of Its Ama'). Extract from the annual of Nihon Kaikoku Suisan Kenkyu-jo (Japanese Institute for the Study of Sea Products), 1952.

KANASAKI, H. *Hekura-jima no Shizen to Jinbun* ('Nature and Man in the Island of Hekura'), extract from the review *Jinbun Chiri* ('Human Geography'), Tokyo, 1949.

BRISTOL, H. *Hatsushima*, in *Japan* (series of 14 photographic monographs), Toppan Press, Tokyo, 1949.

HAAR, F. *Mermaids of Japan*, Pasadena, 1954. (Illustrated album about the Ama, with special reference to those of Onjuku in the Boso peninsula.)

*Distribution of*
*to Professor K. Ya*

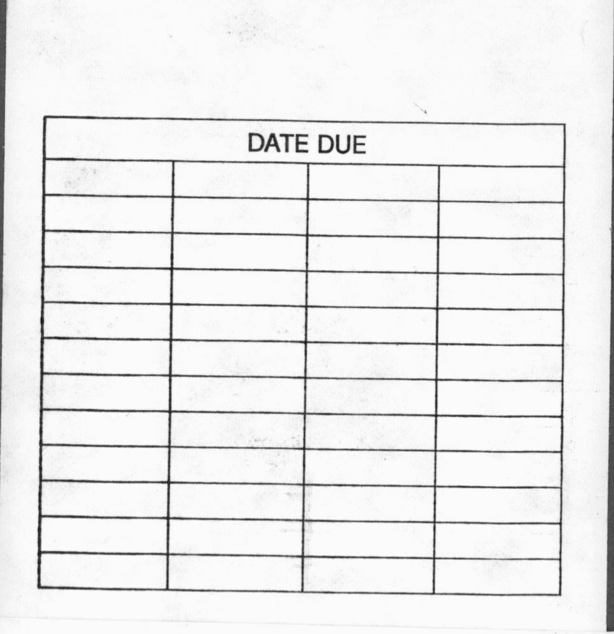